A SHETLAND
Childhood

A SHETLAND Childhood

Memories of the 1950s by
Catherine Emslie

The Shetland Times Ltd.
Lerwick,
2017

A Shetland Childhood

Memories of the 1950s

First published 2017.

ISBN 978-1-910997-11-6

A CIP catalogue record for this book is available from the British Library.

Printed and published by
The Shetland Times Ltd.
Gremista, Lerwick, Shetland, ZE1 0PX.

Dedicated to Calthorpe, Sarah, Alice, Peter and my late sister Robina for their encouragement; to Maureen, Rory, Ian, Richard, Alison, Don and Magi for their help in the carrying out of the task I'd set myself. Special thanks to Vivian, Duncan, Alan, Willie, Elizabeth, Mary, Alma, the Rev. H. R. Bowes and members of the Peebles and Innerleithen Writers' Circle, and of Lerwick Writers' Group.

Preface

This book is about the way of life I knew as a youngster in Shetland in the 1950s. Mostly it is based on my own memories of real events, described from my own perspective as a child at the time, though some chapters deal with family stories as told to me by my parents.

My main reason for writing is to attempt to capture a way of life that has long gone and, in so doing, provide some insight for my Glaswegian nieces into the life and experiences of former generations of their family.

Catherine Emslie

Contents

*I'd like to say that I remember my earliest days when I first
lived in Burra, my parents young, my sister not yet born, but I don't.
My first definite memories are of our subsequent life in Scalloway.
I do, however, have many memories of return visits to Burra.*

But and Ben

"But and ben, but and ben, you were always running but and ben," Auntie Etta likes to tell me when I visit the old house. At night, she lights me a candle before I head along the passage to one of the small bedrooms and follows me to make sure the candle is safe when I blow it out. The moon shining on the back of the house finds a path between the curtains to make dancing patterns on the V-lined wall beside my bed. The light also catches the framed picture that hangs just inside the bedroom door. It is of a polar bear on all fours drifting alone on an ice floe over a bright blue sea, set against an angry orange sky. It is not a comforting picture. I dislike the unnatural colouring and wonder if the sea and the sky can ever look quite like that.

Auntie Etta tells me that my father bought the picture in Iceland when he was in the Navy. He'd been called up not long after he married my mother and they had set up home in this very house. This makes me think about the ben-end, the room through the wall where my parents and I lived before moving to Scalloway. It is now my grandfather's bedroom and I wonder where he slept when we lived here.

My father says we moved because the house was getting too small for all of us and he's probably right, but I wish we'd stayed. Maybe then I would know more about the things Etta talks about and my memories would be complete.

"But and ben, you were always running but and ben," she repeats. Ready to welcome sleep, I almost believe I can remember. I imagine a restless, dark-haired, toddling child stumbling through the wood-lined passage that runs the length of the house. I see her, me, already at the but door. In my mind's eye I am wearing a white dress, perhaps the same crumpled one now worn by my doll. I reach up with both hands to turn the smooth doorknob of the wooden door and burst into the room all smiles, in expectation of an affectionate welcome from grandfather and aunt.

With Auntie Etta.

CHAPTER TWO

This chapter begins in our house in Scalloway and may even contain my first real memory. As it starts, I am three years old.

Special Delivery

Dad and I were ready in good time.

"See if he's turned up yet," Dad suggested.

I stood on a stool and pushed aside the lace curtains that covered the lower half of the window. Very soon, a shiny black car appeared and slowed to a stop at our gate.

"He's here," I called.

Dad looked out. He could see over the curtains. "It's Hindie," he said, and helped me down from the stool.

I was pleased; I liked Hindie. He always had a friendly word for us when we travelled on his buses. This, however, was a special occasion, so we had hired one of his cars.

As Dad and I walked towards the gate, Hindie was standing on the roadway, yellow duster in hand, polishing the chrome and glass headlights. He then moved round to rub at an invisible smudge on the back door before holding it open for us.

I climbed in eagerly and slid right across the seat to leave plenty of room for Dad. I sat back, my feet out in front of me, well above floor level so that the buckles of my Clarks sandals would not scratch the seat. I spread my hands out beside me, fingertips pressed into the upholstery testing its padded comfort, and looked around. The leather and polished wood of the interior hinted to me of luxury and glamour. In the roof was a light, covered in glass. I wondered if it too would be polished before we left. I reached out towards the handles for the door and the window. They were smooth and cool to the touch, but I knew better than to operate them. Then I craned my neck to see into the front of the car, all shining dials and fancy levers. I was going to enjoy this trip.

"What do you think of the new car then, Catherine?"

I looked into the driver's mirror. Hindie was watching me.

"Is this a new one?" I asked.

"Fairly new," he replied. "Do you like it?"

"Mm-mm," I said, then turned to Dad. "Why don't we have a car?" I asked.

Dad just laughed as Hindie started the engine.

He drove at his usual sedate pace, down the road, around the tight corner, past the chapel and onto the main street. Soon we were clear of Scalloway. The engine made a different sound as we toiled up the Scord. Dad and Hindie talked of herring, crans, spents and nets while I looked out the window. I saw the castle with the houses beyond, stretching to the west hill. In the foreground lay the East Voe and the pier. Several fishing boats were tied up at the quayside where I could also make out parked lorries, among them the familiar brown ones belonging to Hindie and his brothers.

From the top of the Scord we began the drive along the back of the hill. To right and left, the land was broken by peat banks, rich brown wounds in the heathery hillside.

The car bounced along. Dad said that was because the road was built on peat. I liked this part of the journey; it reminded me of being in a boat. After a bit, the road dipped towards the Brig o' Fitch from where we caught a glimpse of sea in the distance, but we turned right and headed uphill instead.

At the top was empty moorland, with little to interest me until the road dropped again and I saw the power station, down by the sea, on the outskirts of Lerwick. Soon we had houses on one side and the harbour below us. I was familiar with the route to the pier and the shops, but Hindie turned off before then. After a bewildering number of streets and corners, we stopped on a slope. Hindie reached for his duster from the glove compartment and both men got out.

I remained in the car and watched Dad walk over to a low building where two women were emerging from a doorway. One of them was all in white and in her arms was some sort of white bundle. The other woman was Mam.

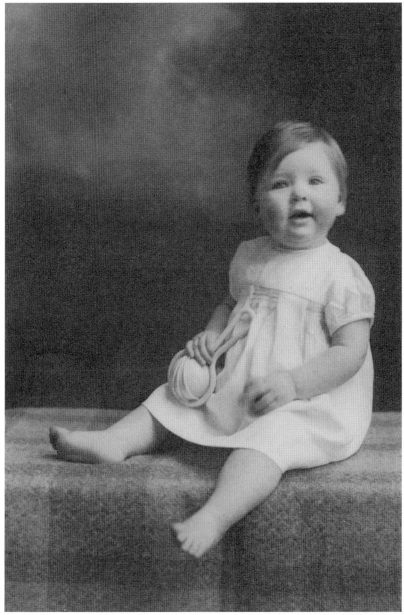

Robina.

Photo by C J Williamson, courtesy of Willie Smith

Dad greeted them and accompanied them to the car. Hindie stopped polishing and opened the front passenger door for Mam. Mam got in, but Hindie did not immediately shut the door. The other woman who had exchanged a few words with Dad, carefully placed the bundle she'd been carrying on Mam's lap.

All smiles, Mam turned to me,

"This is your peerie sister," she said. I'd seen babies before, but I leant forward for a better view.

"What's her name?"

"Robina." My mother was glowing proudly.

"That's a funny name," I said.

"It's my name," she replied.

I was puzzled. "But you're Ruby," I said.

Dad was still explaining that names could be shortened when the car started for home.

As we drew up at our front door, I said to Hindie, "I do like the car. I wish we could have one like it."

His response surprised me. "I'll let your Dad have it," he said, "if you'll give us your little sister."

I considered the offer. Hindie and his wife had no children, but surely he wasn't serious. Dad, at any rate, seemed amused at the idea.

"No," I said, "I think we'll keep her."

CHAPTER THREE

Schoolgirl

"But I'm just four," I said.

"You're nearly five and they say you can start school now at Easter," Mam replied.

"But Vivian's not going."

"Vivian's not five till July," Mam explained, and that was that.

The next morning Mam helped me into my navy gymslip. I liked its new smell as it was pulled on over my head. Later, she held my gabardine raincoat for me. Before putting my arm in, I hesitated, fascinated by the way the lining of coat and hood shone two different colours.

"The sleeve, Catherine," Mam said.

Once I was into the coat and it was buttoned and buckled, I picked up my schoolbag. It wasn't heavy as there wasn't much to put in it, just a pencil case and a paper bag containing a Mowat's muffin and jam: my piece. There was even a separate compartment for the piece, on the front of the bag where the fastenings were. As I thrust my arms through the straps and shrugged the bag into position on my back, Mam held my hood out of the way.

"If it rains," she said, "you can put the hood up. You can't do that if it's stuck behind your schoolbag."

"Is it raining?" I asked, but she was busy getting ready to take Robina next door where Auntie Jessie would look after her.

It was a long way to school; halfway up our road we turned right and headed for Lovers' Lane, a steep footpath that would provide us with a short cut. I ran on and reached the top of the lane first. We often came this way on a Sunday afternoon walk when it was quiet, but today was different; lots of big boys and girls jostled one another down the slope while the youngest ones stayed close to their mothers. As Mam caught up with me, I took her hand.

Both sides of the lane were fenced in, but on the right hand side there was nothing much, apart from a house at the top then grass and trees below. The other side of the lane was more open, being mostly taken up with Sheepie's park, where I had seen ponies and cows as well as sheep.

A burn ran through the park and I wondered if Mam would let me stop at the foot of the slope where the burn disappeared underground. Mam said it re-emerged at the right hand side of the lane where the weeping willows were, overgrown and mysterious. We didn't have time to stop properly so I was allowed a quick look only into the trees; I could hear the water, but, as usual, there was no sign of the burn. After that, the lane rose gently to connect with the road that led to the school.

The school sat at the top of the Mill Brae, on the outskirts of Scalloway, where I'd passed it many times either on walks to the East Voe or in the bus going to Lerwick. The main building, with an adjoining schoolhouse, stood in its own grounds, surrounded by a high brown wall, but Mam and Dad had told me that my classroom was in a different building.

Mam kept a tight hold of my hand as we made our way along the pavement. We still had Sheepie's park on our left; it stretched as far as the school and on to Berry where Sheepie lived, though I'd never seen him. Mam pointed across the park to where two buildings stood on their own.

"The nearer one is the canteen where you go for milk at playtime," she said. "Your classroom is in the next building, the white one."

For a time, we had a clear view of this second building; it was long and narrow with windows along the side, but as the road took us nearer to the school grounds, we lost sight of it altogether.

As we reached the surrounding wall of the school, we became aware of voices, shrill and insistent. The wall was too high to see over, so I let go of Mam's hand and ran ahead to where a metal barrier on the outside edge of the pavement marked the entrance to the school grounds.

With a look back to ensure Mam was still on her way, I went through the large green-painted wooden gate. Just then, a boy walked past and I watched as he headed for the playground to my left where I could see youngsters playing, squabbling and chasing one another – but there were no girls. Mam now caught up with me.

"There are no lasses," I said.

"Round this way," she replied, taking my hand again and guiding me into a larger play area to the right. In here, the noise was less high-pitched, but louder, as older boys with deeper voices rushed round, their feet pounding noisily on the tarred surface. I looked up at Mam.

"The girls' playground is just here," she said, leading me through a gap in a dividing wall. With all ages sharing the one space, the girls' playground was just as busy and just as full of sound and movement as the boys' had been.

I kept hold of Mam's hand as we made our way across the playground to reach a large metal gate that stood open in the far wall. Not far now; the long white building was once again in sight. One final gateway and we were almost at the door.

Once inside, we turned towards the cloakroom with its yellow paint and rows of pegs where Miss Laurenson was waiting for us. She had left the classroom door open and I could see that a few pupils were already at their desks. I'd expected to go straight in, but first Miss Laurenson had to show Mam and me which peg was mine before requesting that I take off my coat and hang it up by the special tag at the back neck. It was a bit fiddly getting it to go over the curly metal, but I managed.

Miss Laurenson then indicated a door at the back of the cloakroom that she said led to the toilets and explained that I'd be allowed in there at playtime, but if I needed to go during lessons I'd have to ask for permission. Next, she took us into the classroom where I wanted to know which desk was mine, but Miss Laurenson had some questions for Mam so she took us over to her own desk first.

"Full name?" she asked.

"Williamina Catherine," Mam answered. I was not happy at this development. I knew I'd been named after my grandmother, Willa Katie, but I didn't care for the first part. My name was Catherine and I hoped Miss Laurenson realised that.

"Date of birth?" Better, I didn't mind this line of questioning.

Soon it was time for Mam to go and, as she left, I was shown to my desk, right at the front. Some children were crying; I didn't know why.

At the start of playtime, Miss Laurenson told us to go to the canteen if we were having school milk. I reached into my schoolbag for my piece. Mam had said that I must have a drink with it, so I knew I'd have to do as Miss

Laurenson had just said. On the way to the canteen door, I passed open windows where steam floated out and disappeared upwards. I could see that the lights were on and hear voices, clattering sounds and running water.

I entered the canteen, a place of activity, cooking smells and steamed-up windows. One of the canteen ladies, in white overall and white hat, was at a serving hatch where she had set out the milk in little coloured plastic mugs. Behind her, I glimpsed the other women busy with large pots and pans.

Most of the seating at the canteen tables was on benches, with a single wooden chair at one end. I felt I couldn't sit on one of those important looking chairs so, after setting my mug carefully on a table, I sat down sideways on a bench and swung my legs round in order to face the table.

The milk had been heated and a skin was growing on it. The paper bag containing my piece had acquired a squashed and stained appearance where the jam had seeped through the bread while it was in my schoolbag, but a Mowat's muffin was my favourite and I devoured it quickly along with the milk before heading outside.

It was time to visit the toilets, but I found them cold and inhospitable. The bolt on the back of the cubicle door was rough to the touch and did not slide easily, and the flush, which worked by a chain, was difficult to operate. For the first time that day, I missed home.

Back in the classroom, I was pleased that Miss Laurenson did call me Catherine as she gave me a slate and slate pencil. I already had a slate at home and liked to draw on it, sometimes even trying to draw patterns like the ones Mam put in the yokes of jumpers, but Miss Laurenson had another purpose in mind. After ensuring her new pupils were facing the blackboard, she used chalk to draw a series of short upright lines, starting at the top each time.

"This is a figure one," she said, "and I want you to copy it on your slates."

Once she was satisfied with the results, she handed out exercise books that were so small, they looked like half a jotter. I opened mine to find squares on each page, but they weren't like the small squares in the jotter Mam kept for dotting down her Fair Isle patterns. These were much bigger and, on the first page, Miss Laurenson had written a figure one in every second box of the top row.

"I want you to copy these all the way down to the foot of the page," she said, "and remember to start each number at the top."

On the way home, I found Vivian waiting for me at her gate.

"What did you do?" she asked.

"A page of ones," I said proudly, and headed for home.

CHAPTER FOUR

Difficulties

We soon learned lots of other numbers and got to know the significance of the figures and dot patterns Miss Laurenson had displayed at the front of the classroom: a single dot for one, two dots for two, and so on. But it was my reading book that I liked best.

"Miss Laurenson says I've to get the book covered," I instructed my parents the first day I brought it home.

Dad had some good strong wrapping paper that he folded and cut to make a neat cover, then he wrote my name on the front. I opened the book and showed Dad a page with lots of coloured pictures and single letters. Miss Laurenson had spoken to my group about these earlier. There was an apple with a little bit of stalk making it the same shape as the large "a" beside it, a curled up cat for "c", a needle with a bit of thread through it making an "n" shape and a soldier standing bolt upright beside a drum for "d". As we worked through the book and learned to recognise sounds and whole words, I began to enjoy the stories of Mother, Father, Ann and Pat.

All went well till two weeks after the Christmas holidays when I developed a chesty cough. One night, I woke to find both my parents at my bedside,

"Try this," Mam said, offering me something from the plate she held. It was a little roll of butter, covered in sugar which she carefully placed in my mouth. As the butter melted into the oily trickle that would sooth the rawness in my throat, I crunched the sugar between my teeth.

"Try and get some sleep now," they said.

Everything was so new and strange that Little Mousie made up his mind to take a little walk to the edge of the cliff and look down. But oh dear! oh dear! the first thing he knew was that he had hurt his toe, and was falling, falling—down! Oh, where was he going? He did not know.

Still, it was fine fun. Once he saw a strange little man no bigger than himself, sitting on a cliff mending shoes. Then he saw a lot of little folk sitting on toad-stools, and when he got

17

close enough, he heard them singing.

'Well, they must be happy. Maybe they are having a party. I think I'll call and see them,' thought Little Mousie. 'This falling isn't half bad when you get used to it.'

CHAPTER FOUR

 JUST at that moment Little Mousie landed safely in a nice bed of soft, green moss. Picking himself up, he rubbed his eyes, for it was quite dark until he became used to it. Then he could see quite well.

Little Mousie now found himself in a long tunnel, at the other end of which was a big, green lamp. He

18

Little Mousie, published by W & R Chambers Ltd., 1951.

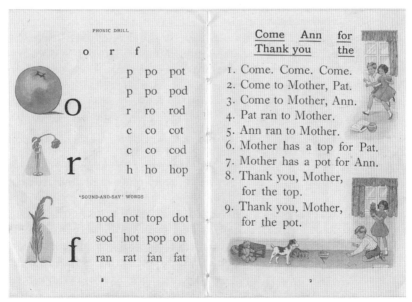

PHONIC DRILL

o r f

p	po	pot
p	po	pod
r	ro	rod
c	co	cot
c	co	cod
h	ho	hop

'SOUND-AND-SAY' WORDS

nod	not	top	dot
sod	hot	pop	on
ran	rat	fan	fat

Come	Ann	for
Thank you		the

1. Come. Come. Come.
2. Come to Mother, Pat.
3. Come to Mother, Ann.
4. Pat ran to Mother.
5. Ann ran to Mother.
6. Mother has a top for Pat.
7. Mother has a pot for Ann.
8. Thank you, Mother, for the top.
9. Thank you, Mother, for the pot.

Reading book, *The Radiant Way, First Step* also published by W & R Chambers Ltd.

In the morning, when Mam came to waken me, she had the thermometer with her. She gave it a good shake before placing it under my arm, with instructions that I keep still and not let it slip out.

When it had been in for the required time, she removed it carefully to squint closely at the small numbers that would tell her what she needed to know.

"You're running a temperature," she said, fussing with the bedclothes. "You'll have to keep warm."

Dr Durham was sent for. His stethoscope was cold on my front and back as he listened to my breathing. After he'd gone, Mam came to tell me I had bronchitis and had to stay in bed. "I'm going to the chemist's for some cough medicine," she added.

The medicine was a deep pink colour which gave the impression of being sweet, but there was a bitter aftertaste. Before putting the top back on the bottle, Mam tried to remove any spills with the edge of a spoon.

Dad blamed my illness on the building my classroom was in. The temporary structure was difficult to heat, the room smelt of damp plasticine and the windows ran with condensation.

"It's not for bairns," he said, "especially infants."

When Dr Durham next came to see me, my favourite book, *Little Mousie*, was lying on the bed. It was a story book that I'd been given as a Sunday School prize. It had full-page coloured pictures and lots of line drawings that I enjoyed colouring in. Little Mousie had great adventures, even flying off to the moon in an aeroplane.

After listening to my chest again, Dr Durham picked up the book and leafed through it.

"Do you like this story?" he asked.

I nodded. "Mam and Dad read it to me," I said.

"Can you read it to me?" he asked, holding out the book.

I took it and turned over the first few pages to where I knew the story started.

"*'Oh dear! but I am tired!' said Little Mousie,*" I began, barely looking at the words. I'd had the book since last summer and it had been read to me so often that I knew lots of it by heart. I even knew when to turn the pages.

As I went on, Dr Durham seemed to be enjoying the story too, but by the fourth page, when Little Mousie was in conversation with the pilot of the plane, my pretend reading began to falter and the doctor said I was to stop.

I had bronchitis three times that winter and was off school four weeks each time: a lot of weeks. It was the month of May before I began to keep better and my attendance picked up, but I was no longer sure that I liked school. When I'd recited bits of *Little Mousie* to Dr Durham, Mam said I was word perfect, but coping with books at school was a different matter.

After my third long absence, Miss Laurenson called my reading group out to the floor, so I got up and stood in line with the others as usual. Once we'd all found the correct page, Miss Laurenson began to read while we followed, tracing our fingers along the lines of print, but this time, so many of the words were unfamiliar, I found it hard to keep up.

This was a shock, but I concentrated hard, knowing that, when she stopped, it would be our turn. We'd each take a few lines at a time and, if I could just work out and memorise what the new words said, before it was my turn, I'd be all right.

However, as I stood there, I quickly became lost in wonder as other pupils read aloud. Where did they get the words? I recognised some of them, but so many of the new words looked the same, that I couldn't work out which made which sound. When my turn came round, I tried to fill in the gaps from memory with my *Little Mousie* trick, but that wasn't enough and the very next day I was put into another reading group.

A few days later, when Mam was shopping at the Street, she met my teacher who told her she'd already moved me into the bottom group, but I was still struggling so much, she thought she might have to take me on my own.

Miss Laurenson still hadn't done that when my folks told me that Mam was going into hospital and Robina and I were going to Hamnavoe.

CHAPTER FIVE

A Change of Scene

Separate Quarters

"When I go into hospital, you're going to Granda's," Mam said. "Auntie Etta'll look after you."

"And Robina?" I enquired.

"She's going to Duke Street. Auntie Maggie'll look after her."

I was pleased we were going to Hamnavoe and didn't mind that it was to different houses.

"What about Dad?" I asked.

"You'll see him at weekends," was the answer.

"I won't be able to go to school," I said.

My mother smiled. "You can go to the Hamnavoe School," she replied.

I wasn't sure what I felt about that. I hadn't attended my own school much, recently; what would I think of someone else's?

New School

Hamnavoe School was smaller than the one in Scalloway though both were junior secondary schools with primary classes as well. I was in a room in the main building which pleased my Dad. It was large and square and jammed with desks. The floor was wooden and the windows set so high in the wall you couldn't see out, except to watch the clouds in the sky.

My new teacher was the headmaster's wife, Mrs McWhirter, whom I already knew as she seemed to be a friend of Auntie Etta. She wasn't like anyone else I'd met, but reminded me of women in the adverts in magazines. She was slim with long hair that was curly at the ends and on top. She wore a greyish-blue costume and a little pale blouse. The jacket was fitted at the waist, and the skirt slim-fitting.

I was used to a single desk with a tip-up seat, but here the desks were for two pupils. Mrs McWhirter put me to sit beside Sandra whose father owned the beef shop opposite the school. My cousin Ann sat in front of us.

Mrs McWhirter gave me a reading book. I looked inside it. It was different from the one I had at Scalloway. It didn't seem to be about Mother and Father and Ann and Pat, nor did it have any full-colour pictures. It had different stories. I recognised the story of the Gingerbread Man from the little line drawings. There he was, running away from a surprised cook, and there he was, being eaten by a fox that was swimming. I'd have liked to colour in the pictures, but didn't think Mrs McWhirter would let me.

"Get a cover put on the book," she said.

I decided to leave that till Dad returned.

Meeting the Boat

Dad was in Lerwick at the herring fishing which meant he'd been away from home since Monday, but this was Saturday so he'd be catching the dennertime bus from Lerwick to the Scalloway pier in good time to catch the half-past-one boat to Hamnavoe. Auntie Etta said we'd eat when Dad arrived, so, while she was cooking, I went to meet the *Tirrick*.

Granda's house stood a bit up from the shore, therefore, to get a clear view of the pier, I had to take the path to lower Duke Street. Duke Street wasn't like the Scalloway streets with lights and pavements; it was simply a path that ran in front of a handful of houses. The duke part was wrong too; apparently some official, who misunderstood what people were saying, had written the name down wrongly. Mam lived there when she was peerie and she told me that it was really named after the ducks people used to keep. Nowadays there were none, only hens. Auntie Maggie had a henhouse right on the sea edge.

There was no sign of the boat yet, but the front door of Auntie Maggie's house was standing open, so I went in through the porch, opened the inner door and stepped into the passage. Auntie Maggie's dog, Dot, a fat little pale-brown body on short legs, appeared, gave a half-hearted bark and waddled towards me, followed by Robina.

"It's Catherine," she half-turned and spoke over her shoulder.

"Come in, Catherine," I heard Auntie Maggie's voice say. "You'll be going to meet the *Tirrick*," she continued, as I followed Robina in but. The dog came too and lay down on its bed in the corner. Robina clambered into one of the chairs, but I didn't feel I had time to sit down so stood, just inside the door.

Auntie Maggie was sitting by the fire, makkin. She was knitting a Fair Isle yoke, a large bag of coloured cloos on the floor beside her seat. Like my mother, she wore a makkin belt that left her forefingers free to manipulate the strands of yarn.

Mam told me the belt allowed you to work quickly. She was more interested in knitting than in reading and had taught me to makk before I went to school, but I still hadn't used a belt. Also like Mam, Auntie Maggie could knit without looking at what she was doing and did so while speaking.

She asked me how I was getting on and was telling me what she and Robina had been up to when it occurred to her to look at the clock. She stopped her story then, pulled the right hand makkin wire out of her belt and said, "Run ben and tell me if you can see the boat."

Sensing some action, Dot pushed himself up and followed me, but lost interest when I didn't head outside. I reached over the deep sill of the ben window to the net curtains, drew them apart and squinted out towards the pier and beyond. The top of the *Tirrick*'s mast, shaped like a plus sign, was visible over the low headland. She would soon be in sight.

I ran back, calling out, "She's coming round The Point now." I was excited; this beat meeting the bus in Scalloway.

Auntie Maggie was already on her feet. She'd been ill when she was little and couldn't walk properly, but taking Robina by the hand, she hobbled towards the door. I followed and, once outside, ran ahead to the end of Duke Street where I stopped beside a cluster of large metal cans, kirns we called them, standing outside Uncle Hancie's milk shop.

Not everyone got their milk from the shop. Auntie Etta got milk from Baabie and Jackie who had a cow at Clate, up past Granda's house. The two women were sisters and we used to see them, dressed always in black with black headscarves, make their way up the road with a large white bucket that would be full of milk on their return, but there weren't enough cows in Burra to provide milk for everyone so Uncle Hancie brought in extra on the *Tirrick*.

The *Tirrick* was his boat and he ran her every day from Scalloway where he lived, to Hamnavoe and back again. It was Auntie Maggie's job

Auntie Maggie and Dot.

to open up the shop and sell the milk for the few hours it took each day. Before closing up, she'd wash out the kirns and place them where I now stood so they could be picked up to go back on the two o'clock boat.

Beyond the milk shop was a road and an open area known as The Beach that spread down to the pier. When my aunt and sister caught up with me, Auntie Maggie said that she and Robina would wait by the milk shop if I wished to continue on to the pier.

The *Tirrick* was in full view now, her black hull low in the water, her deck crowded with dark figures emerging from the cabin. These were the herring fishermen returning for the weekend, dressed in their go-shores: cloth caps worn with navy serge suits over hand-knitted navy jumpers.

In Scalloway, the *Tirrick*'s arrivals and departures went largely unnoticed, but here in Hamnavoe, where most houses overlooked the voe, people either watched the comings and goings from their front porches or wandered down to meet the boat.

I joined those lingering at the head of the pier, hoping that I wouldn't have to venture onto the big wooden pier itself where, in places, the wood had rotted away to leave gaps. I'd never heard of anyone fall through, but my great fear was of tumbling into the sunless water below: water that, confined by wooden uprights, could be heard swinkling angrily underneath.

I needn't have worried. Today the conditions were right for the *Tirrick* to come in to the Staney Pier that lay next to the big pier. As soon as the boat came alongside, the men began to disembark and I ran to meet Dad.

Together, we set off for Granda's, picking up Robina on the way.

A Cover for my Book

In the afternoon, Dad took us to Robbie's shop. It was unlike most of the Scalloway shops; it didn't even have a sign. It was in one half of a wooden building with concrete steps to the door. You could buy lots of different things there and it was always open, even at night. It used to belong to Dad's Uncle Jamie and Dad told us he'd worked there when he first left school. He said he'd had to cut bacon with a knife instead of a bacon machine. I don't know what the inside of the shop looked like then, but now the V-lined walls were brightly painted, and the counter, a shiny varnished brown.

There were always men in the shop, some of them sitting, the others standing around. Occasionally they'd buy a bag of sweeties or a box of matches, but they weren't simply customers; this was their meeting place. They hung round yarning, sometimes including those who were waiting to be served. Everyone knew everyone else so there was lots of banter among the chat.

When we went in, some people spoke to Dad and asked for Mam. Others spoke to Robina and me.

"What do you think of the Hamnavoe School, Catherine?" someone said.

I wasn't sure what I thought of any school. "We're buying brown paper for my books," I replied.

Back at Granda's, Dad covered my reading book and printed my name on it.

"I can't write my name," I said.

"Never mind," he answered, "if you need to, just you copy what I've put here." I looked closely at what he'd written. I knew it as far as c-a-t, but after that it got complicated. Why did it need so many letters?

At school on Monday, when Mrs McWhirter gave me a piece of paper to work on, she expected to have to help me with my name. Instead, I got out my reading book and proudly copied what Dad had written.

I had just replaced the reading book in my desk when Mrs McWhirter appeared at my side.

"That's not correct," she said and took the page from me. She used my rubber then wrote her version of my name. There was a 'y' in it. I wondered what Dad would have said.

The Coronation

Newspapers and magazines were full of pictures of the Queen and her family. I was fascinated by the long dresses and the fancy robes, by the horse-drawn coaches and the large crowds. If Mam had been at home she'd have commented on Princess Anne in her pretty dress and her gold curls; the princess was just one day older than Robina so Mam took a particular interest in her.

At school, Mrs McWhirter spoke to us about the Royal Family and explained that all the fuss was because the King had died last year and now his elder daughter was being crowned Queen. She said it was called a Coronation and showed us a colour picture of the Queen sitting alone, a large crown on her head and a long pole in her hand.

The best bit though was that all the schoolchildren were to have a special present. Unfortunately, it wasn't made clear where the present was to come from and this bothered me. The Queen herself wouldn't be bringing it, but the people involved might think I was still at my own school, in Scalloway. My present could easily go to the wrong place. Would they keep it for me?

I needn't have worried, when the gifts were handed out at the end of the school day, I was included. I rushed off to show Auntie Etta and Granda right away. There were two things: a Mars bar and a little enamelled brooch shaped like a red, white and blue bow with a crown at its centre.

"They must have sent mine specially on the *Tirrick*," I said.

Sports Day

One day, Mrs McWhirter told us we were all going to the Fraser Park in Scalloway. "It's the annual sports competition between the Hamnavoe and Scalloway schools." she said.

My cousin Robert and the other good runners among the older children began practising keenly; it was important to do well against Scalloway.

On the day of the sports, Mrs McWhirter lined us up in pairs, putting me with Ann before we walked along to the *Tirrick*. Although he wasn't always on board, Uncle Hancie was there today, along with Andrew, the ferryman, to help us from the pier onto the boat. I liked going on the *Tirrick*, especially if I could be in the wheelhouse, but, for this trip, I had to do as Mrs McWhirter said and that meant travelling below, in the cabin.

We followed her along the deck to the stern where a seat of slatted brown wood stood opposite the entrance to the cabin. Mrs McWhirter went first, down the short fat ladder with the wide treads. At the bottom, she turned, so as to keep an eye on us as we made it onto the boards of the cabin floor. Some children were already seated, squashed onto the cushioned bench seats that ran along each side.

"Sit here please." Mrs McWhirter indicated seats beside the steps.

Ann and I squeezed into our places. Opposite us, through cabin windows streaked with salty deposits, we could just make out the land above Bakkaburn, but even that limited view was soon obscured by the bare legs and knee socks of the older children who were allowed to stay on deck.

Someone pulled the heavy, brown wooden hatch into position over our heads, leaving the cabin open to the back only. The engine whined,

Uncle Hancie in the door of the *Tirrick*'s wheelhouse. *Photo by C J Williamson, courtesy of Willie Smith*

blue smoke blew round the stern and fumes drifted inside. Quiet with anticipation, we heard the soft thump of a painter landing on the deck. Andrew's dungareed legs came into view. He checked that everything was as it should be at the stern and the *Tirrick* backed off from the pier. As we turned towards the mouth of the voe, Ann and I twisted round to be sure of getting a glimpse of the lighthouse.

The *Tirrick* rolled as she rounded The Point and passed Atla Holm. Ann and I giggled and bounced up and down in our seats; these were the bits we liked. We wouldn't be whisked off by Mrs McWhirter "for some fresh air" and a miserable spell on the slatted brown seat.

The Firths were calm that day. After a bit, Ann and I began looking round for a glimpse of the Green Holm, a small round hill sitting in the sea, green as its name and fringed with black rocks. No-one lived there, but we were close enough to catch sight of some sheep. Not long after that, the *Tirrick* slowed; we were in the voe at Scalloway and approaching the shore.

The engine screeched as the boat manoeuvred into position. We heard the lapping of water on the stones of Blacksness Pier. Andrew appeared briefly. He threw the aft painter ashore, slid open the brown hatch and was gone.

The *Tirrick* was secured. Legs and knee socks disappeared from our view as the older pupils filed ashore first. When it was our turn, Ann and I followed Mrs McWhirter up the cabin steps.

At the top, she stopped by the brown seat to wait till the cabin emptied. "You go on," she said. We turned along the deck. The tide was so far out that the deck was below the level of the pier, but I spotted Uncle Hancie and his white hat, already ashore. Andrew was still on board, standing by the L-shaped brown box that was both seat in the wheelhouse and welcome set of steps on deck. Andrew took my hand as I clambered to the top of the box. The next bit was tricky, but Uncle Hancie took my other hand and my arm to assist me over the treacherous gap between boat and pier.

"Mrs McWhirter's class, over here," Mrs McWhirter called out.

Ann and I took our place in front of the other children, well away from the edge of the pier. Some boys pushed in front of us, but Mrs McWhirter moved them back.

When everyone was in line, Ann and I led the school up the pier, past the castle, round Wilfie's corner, along to Clement's studio, down to the Burn Beach and onto the main street. I was so proud. Mrs McWhirter might not believe I could get my name right, but she knew I could find the Fraser Park.

CHAPTER SIX

*After three weeks at the Hamnavoe School, I returned
to my own school for the last two weeks of term.*

School Trip

"Stand still," Mam said, "while I get your ribbon in."

"We won't be in the school for the whole day today," I responded, before attempting to turn my head to tell her why, but Mam's grip on my hair was strong. "We're going to the castle," I continued, "Miss Laurenson said."

"I know;" Mam replied; "I hope you like it," but she sounded doubtful.

The castle was easily the tallest building in Scalloway and one of the first things you noticed when you came over the Scord. It stood close to the sea at a point where the East Voe met the main voe. I'd passed it lots of times on the way to Blacksness pier or to Hay's shop with Mam. Yesterday, Miss Laurenson had told us a bit about the castle and Earl Patrick who built it and, even if Mam weren't enthusiastic, I was looking forward to seeing inside.

After we had lined up in twos, my class at the front and Primary 2 behind, we left the infant room and followed Miss Laurenson out of the school grounds.

"Stay together," she instructed, as we followed her along the pavement. When we got to the old church that was the school gym hall, Miss Laurenson led us across the road and into Castle Street.

"There's no pavement here;" she pointed out, before adding firmly, "you must stay well in to the side of the road."

Castle Street was on a slope with a few houses on one side and a good view over the Bool Green and East Voe to a handful of houses scattered along the hill, on the other. It was hard-going, coping with the slope and

Top: *I hadn't realised the castle was quite as tall.* Above left: Crumbling stairs. Above right: The overhead fireplace.

trying to stay in line. After a bit, Miss Laurenson stopped us to sort out the stragglers before we moved on again to reach the white house, known as Howarth's, at the top. Ahead of us, down a shorter, but steeper and more twisty bit of roadway, lay the castle.

Whether it was the relief of no longer having to climb or the sight of our destination, I didn't know, but we soon covered the ground to arrive at a gate in the castle wall. This gate was well away from the road and Miss Laurenson left us there while she fetched the key from Annslea, a nearby house standing on a bend in the road, above the pier.

Miss Laurenson led us through the gate where the ground continued on a downward slope before it reached the castle itself. On the way round to the door, I glanced upwards; yellowish-brown walls blotted out sight of everything else. I hadn't realised the castle was quite as tall.

The large iron key turned easily in the lock, the studded wooden door swung open and Miss Laurenson ushered us inside. We were in a passageway, gloomier and colder than the weather outside. Ahead of us was a wide staircase and on our left, an arched doorway where Miss Laurenson said we'd start our tour.

She went first then turned to help each of us down a set of rough stone steps into a small room. It was a sort of dungeon with an arched recess at one end where Miss Laurenson said prisoners had sometimes been kept, but I was more intrigued by a hole in the outside wall that she said was for shooting at unwelcome visitors.

Safely back up the steps, we were led along a corridor to an empty room at the end where there wasn't much to see, so we were soon out in the passageway again, feet crunching on shingle as we went. Next door was the castle kitchen; it was similar in size to the previous room, but with more to interest us.

At one end, a metal grille was set into the floor. I went over for a closer look, but there wasn't enough light to see clearly into the opening below. Set into the opposite wall was an enormous fireplace. Miss Laurenson told us that was where cooking had been done and encouraged us to have a closer look, so I ran over. Above the noise of chat and movement on the stone floor, I heard another sound, soft yet throaty and accompanied by the unmistakable fluttering of wings. I looked up inside the chimney in time to catch sight of a pigeon alighting on some stonework high above my head. I'd expected the chimney to be round inside, like the chimney pots at home, but it had straight sides narrowing to a rectangular slot where there was daylight, a long way up.

Miss Laurenson then called us back across the room. Insisting that we stay perfectly quiet, she picked up a small stone and dropped it through the grating in the floor. Listening intently, we heard a splash; the stone had landed in water. The opening in the floor was the castle's water supply: their very own well.

Next, we went up the wide stairway. It was hard work as the steps were so high. On the way up, Miss Laurenson stopped us beside a small cave-like room where she said Earl Patrick had locked his family when the king's soldiers came to arrest him. We couldn't go into the room as there were no steps, so after a quick look, we continued up the stairs.

At the top, we stepped into daylight; there was no longer a roof overhead.

"This is the Great Hall," Miss Laurenson said. We were in a large room with lots of windows and two fireplaces. Then I noticed another fireplace, but this one was set into the wall above our heads. After allowing us a few minutes to take in our surroundings, Miss Laurenson explained that there were two storeys missing and drew our attention to marks along the wall that she said was where the next floor up had been. The overhead fireplace had been in a room in the next level up.

"I'll show you where the stairs were," she said, and asked us to follow her towards a doorway in the corner. "There's just room," she went on, "for a few of you at a time."

On the other side of the doorway, a few badly-worn steps marked the bottom of the old staircase, but beyond that, the stairs had crumbled away so much they no longer provided a foothold. One at a time, Miss Laurenson helped us onto the lower steps. When it was my turn, I was able to look up to where the walls rose, forming an enclosed circular shape.

"This is called a turret," she explained to the group, "and you can see where the stairs continued." High above our heads, narrow stone ridges wound their way up the turret wall.

When we were all back in the Great Hall, Miss Laurenson asked us to follow her across the Hall to an archway in the opposite corner. This led to another spiral staircase, but one composed of smooth wedge-shaped steps twisting their way upwards and out of sight. Miss Laurenson went first, telling us to keep close to the wall where the treads were at their widest.

At the top, she directed us into a small room where she pointed out a rectangular opening high up in the wall. It resembled a cupboard without doors, but it was in there, she told us, that Earl Patrick had hidden from the soldiers.

Back in the Great Hall, Miss Laurenson stood at one of the windows where she lifted each of us up in turn so we could see the view across the road to the pier and the voe beyond. We then headed down the main stairs and out through the wooden door, but our visit wasn't quite over.

Instead of taking us back to the gate the way we'd come, Miss Laurenson led us round in the opposite direction so she could point out the turret where we'd climbed the spiral staircase.

"If you look straight up from the top of the turret," she said, "you'll see a long narrow opening in the wall. That's Earl Patrick's hiding place and, when the soldiers saw pipe smoke coming from there, they went inside and arrested him."

Back at school, we got to draw a picture of the castle. I drew my favourite bit: the kitchen with its water supply and large grate.

Mam was at the sink, filling the kettle, when I got home.

"What did you think of the castle?" she asked.

"Good," I said, "we went up a spiral staircase."

"Was that what you liked best?"

"No, that was downstairs," I replied, looking round, "they had a well in their kitchen."

At one end, a metal grille was set into the floor.

CHAPTER SEVEN

Spangles

I don't know what woke me: the sound of the car, the click of the front gate or the front door being opened and closed in a way intended not to disturb, but whichever it was, I was wide awake to the sound of someone creeping up the stairs. It would be Davie back from his squad meeting.

I prodded Robina to see if she was awake. In a little while we'd see the glow of Davie's cigarette as he passed our room in the dark on his way to the spare bedroom.

Davie was our big cousin who had lodged with us ever since Auntie Jessie went back to Hamnavoe. He was good at fixing things which, with Dad away so much, was a great help to Mam. Robina and I also enjoyed having him around; we didn't have a car, so an occasional trip in Davie's was a great treat, but the most regular treats we got were the packets of Spangles he bought us. We even had a special place to keep them in a corner of the but window where, because of their square shape, the packets stacked up neatly, one on top of another, contrasting layers half-hidden behind the gold-coloured curtain.

There was the bluey-green of the Acid Drops packets; the fresh white and pink of the mint ones; the dark red that told us the contents were blackcurrant-flavoured; and the dingy yellow used to package those I liked least, the Old English variety. My favourites were the original Spangles, a selection of fruit flavours in a red and silver striped packet: tangy green and yellow ones, the sweeter orange and red ones, and blackcurrant, each flavour presented in a different colour of waxed paper so you could tell which was which.

Spangles could be enjoyed in different ways too. Most could be crunched loudly and confidently to produce a satisfying rush of flavour. On the other hand, the Acid Drops variety required an affectation of distaste where you screwed up your mouth and eyes in a way that belied the enjoyment you felt. Those of a deeper hue would rapidly transfer their colour to your tongue and teeth, but these versatile sweets didn't always demand attention, their flat shape and rounded corners enabling all but the Acid Drops to melt slowly and unobtrusively in a corner of the mouth. In fact, this last method often gave rise to competitions between Robina and me to see whose Spangle could last longer.

"What are you doing?" I asked Mam. Usually when I came home from school, she was makkin, but today she was working with a kind of red ribbon while something in white fabric lay beside her on the chair.

"It's for Davie," she said.

"Davie!"

Before I could ask any more, she went on, "It's for Up-Helly-Aa."

"But what is it? What's he dressing up as?"

"I don't know," she said, "this ribbon has to be sewn on to these trousers."

That's what the white cloth was. I had a closer look and found she'd already tacked some of the ribbon along the full length of one of the trouser legs and was measuring out some more.

The only person I knew with a red stripe on his trousers was the postman, but that stripe was much thinner and, besides, his trousers weren't white.

"Who wears white breeks?" I asked.

Mam shook her head and directed me upstairs to change out of my school clothes.

It was sassermaet for tea that night, but Robina and I had our minds on other things, bombarding Davie with questions.

"Davie, what are you going as?"

"Where did you get the white breeks?"

"Why a red stripe? Are you a postman?"

As he was giving nothing away, it was time for a change of tack.

"What about the procession; are we going?"

"If it's a fine night," Mam said, and that was that.

On the last Tuesday of January, it was hard to concentrate at school. I kept an eye on the window, fearful of pouring rain or worse: anything that would cause Mam to cancel our trip to Lerwick. Eventually, the bell rang and Miss Laurenson felt she had to remind us there was no school tomorrow.

"Did she think we'd forgotten?" someone asked, as we headed home as quickly as possible.

The weather being judged fine, Mam was ready with instructions for what we had to wear at night. "Trousers," she said, "and jumpers. You can put on your allovers as well before we leave."

After tea, it was warm pixies and coats for us, while Mam dressed in a thick coat and a woollen headsquare. Dad wasn't coming with us; the fishermen didn't and Davie was already in Lerwick.

"Can we take some sweeties?" Robina asked. "We've plenty of Spangles."

"Take some that have already been opened," Mam said, as we pulled aside the curtain to make our choice. Robina selected a half-packet of mint ones. I was tempted by the Acid Drops, but none of those was open so I stuck with my favourites.

"Hurry up," Mam said, "if you want a seat in the bus."

Dad came to the door with us and looked at the sky, the way he did, and told us it would be cold, but should remain dry. We wished him goodnight; he had to get up again at the back of two so would be in bed long before we were home.

In the glow of the street lights, we were aware of others on the move, walking purposefully down the road or joining us at the post box corner, all heading in the same direction to turn right at the chapel and on to the Co-op corner. Opposite the Co-op, Georgeson and Moore's bus was at its stance. It would leave five minutes before ours and already had a good number of passengers on board, shadowy figures glimpsed through windows that were already steamed-up against the cold night air.

We continued along to Williamson's where Hindie's bus waited and, once on board, we began to speculate once more about Davie's costume.

"Mam, you must know; you helped him with it."

"You know as much as I do," she replied, "you saw the trousers with the red stripe."

Just as it was dawning on us that further pestering would yield no more information, Georgeson and Moore's bus drove past, the steamy windows relieved here and there by a clearer arc of glass where a hand, or perhaps a sleeve, had provided its owner with a view of the world. We turned our attention to the front of our bus where the clock with the rectangular face hung, its hands dragging their way through the remaining five minutes.

We got off the bus at the foot of Harbour Street and hurried up the brae. At the junction with Market Street, we turned in the direction of the Town Hall, its clock face warning that it wouldn't be long now till lighting up.

"Are we going to the War Memorial?" I asked.

"If there's still space," Mam replied.

"Will we see Davie?" Robina wondered.

"We'll have to hope there aren't too many squads in white breeks," Mam said.

As we neared the Town Hall, Mam guided us across the road to where she had spotted a convenient gap among the spectators at the memorial, and so we found ourselves with a good view down the Town Hall Brae and across to King Harald Street where the turning movement would take place. There would be plenty of opportunity to watch out for Davie.

Time for a sweetie before it starts, I thought, and retrieved the half-eaten packet of Spangles from my pocket. In the strange orange glow of the street lights, I could still see that the packet was striped, but it had lost much of its colour. After removing one of my mittens in order to prise a sweetie out of the packet, I held it up and squinted to see if I could tell which flavour it was, but the wavy stripes on the waxed paper looked black under the lights. I unwrapped it, placed it in my mouth and just as the strawberry flavour was revealed, the street lights went out and an appreciative murmur ran through the crowd. Next, the whoosh of the Verey light drew our eyes momentarily skywards while below us in the Lower Hillhead, the darkness gave way to the spreading glow from newly-lit torches.

"Not long now," I said. Mam agreed, a smile in her voice.

As more torches were lit, sparks rose into the blackness above, burned brightly then vanished among traces of smoke. The pipe band struck up and, in the torchlight, we got our first glimpse of the red-and-white striped galley as it glided past, a proud Guizer Jarl on board. Alongside, on the roadway, marched the Jarl Squad, but we knew they'd be dressed as

Vikings; we were more interested in finding out what Davie's squad would look like.

There was more music, from the brass band this time, and intermittent singing of Up-Helly-A' songs, but it was the guizers' costumes that received most of our attention. Indians, clowns, judges, and those defying description paraded in front of us until, at last, we gasped and pointed.

There they were: a handful of men dressed in white shirts worn with smart bow ties, and white trousers with the expected red stripe, but that wasn't what caught our attention most. Two members of the squad were wearing over their suits, a tall box-like arrangement with horizontal stripes and large lettering that ran from top to bottom to spell one word – *Spangles*.

CHAPTER EIGHT

Winning Ways

"It isn't for bairns," Mam said.

We were at Granda's and she was getting ready to attend a do with Dad in the Bridge End Hall. I found Dad in but, with Granda.

"Why can't I go?" I asked, but Dad only repeated what Mam had said.

"Who will be there, then?" I enquired.

"The crew and anyone else that's invited, I expect," he said, though that didn't really help.

I knew that the crew he mentioned were the men he'd been to Lowestoft with, on the *Jessie Sinclair*, but I didn't even know much about them. The skipper, Bob Williamson, had two brothers in Scalloway: Tammie, who lived near to us, and Gideon, our new next door neighbour since Auntie Jessie moved back to Burra, but they weren't on the *Jessie Sinclair*. Another brother, Johnnie, was, and Dad had pointed him out in photos of the crew.

In one photo, the crew was shown smiling to the camera from the bow of the boat with the name clearly visible, but the photo that I found most intriguing was from *The Fishing News* and showed the men at the posh Prunier restaurant in London. A table, covered in a white cloth than almost reached the floor, ran the whole width of the photo. At this table two important looking men sat, close to where a woman stood. She was the only woman in the photo and was very smart, dressed in black and wearing glasses. Dad said she was Madame Prunier who owned the restaurant, but there was no doubt that the main focus of the shot was the *Jessie Sinclair*'s men.

Prunier Herring Trophy winners, 1954. *Back:* Willie Goodlad (Dad), Jamsie Christie, George Cogle, Bob Williamson, Sinclair Goodlad, Charlie Bruce Christie. *Front:* Johnnie Williamson, Tammie Inkster, Willie Laurenson, Geordie Hunter.

All dressed up in their suits and collars and ties, they formed a line right across the photo, though Bob was on his own in front of the table while his men stood with Madame Prunier behind it. Looking along the line of men, I could see that Dad was the tallest, though some of the others were nearly as tall, and it looked as if Johnnie and Bob were the smallest. Bob was holding up a weather vane that Dad had told me was intended for the *Jessie Sinclair*'s mast. It was in the shape of a herring to show that the *Jessie Sinclair* was this year's winner of the Prunier trophy, awarded annually to the boat that had the largest single catch during the East Anglian herring season. On a small table beside Bob was the trophy itself, depicting a hand grasping a herring. This was the first time a Shetland boat had won and the men were now to be honoured at Bridge End.

"Are you sure there won't be any bairns?" I tried again.

Dad shook his head. "You and Robina are to stay here with Auntie Etta and Granda."

Just then Mam came into the room. She was now wearing her winter coat over her dress.

Dad stood up, put on his jacket and cap and they were heading for the door when Auntie Etta appeared out of the kitchen. "We'll hear all about it in the morning," she said, and they were gone, out into the December night.

All dressed up in their suits and collars and ties, they formed a line right across the photo.

Photo by Graphic House, London

I spent the rest of the time before bedtime looking through the mementos Dad had brought back from Lowestoft. First there was the shiny silver ashtray he had been presented with at the restaurant. It had the year and Dad's name on it above a picture of a herring with Prunier Trophy written across it in capital letters. Then there were photos, newspapers, post cards showing the restaurant inside and out, the menu, the invitation to the Prunier restaurant and even the envelope in which it had been sent to Dad. It hadn't been sent to Scalloway, but was addressed to Dad, care of the LHD at the Lowestoft Herring Market and it said it was for Luncheon. Dad had also brought the menu home with him, but it wasn't in English. It was in French he said, just like the label of an HP Sauce bottle.

I picked up a news item Dad had torn from a newspaper: *Shetland boat should win the 'Prunier'* it read.

"What does this mean?" I asked.

It was Auntie Etta who replied, "They were told they were likely to win even before the competition closed," she said.

"There was nothing doing by then," Granda added, "lots of the boats had left." Then, indicating the scrap of paper in my hand, he went on, "It says there it had got to the stage that thirteen boats were landing just eighteen and a half cran among them."

Above: My father's commemorative ashtray. Left: Invitation to the trophy presentation luncheon. Below: *Dad had also brought the menu home with him, but it wasn't in English.*

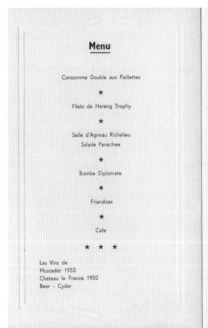

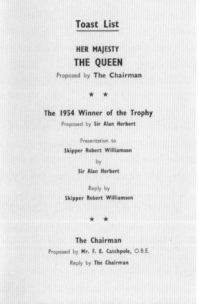

Menu

Consomme Double aux Paillettes

★

Filets de Hareng Trophy

★

Selle d'Agneau Richelieu
Salade Panachee

★

Bombe Diplomate

★

Friandises

★

Cafe

★ ★ ★

Les Vins de
Muscadet 1953
Chateau la France 1950
Beer - Cyder

Toast List

HER MAJESTY
THE QUEEN
Proposed by **The Chairman**

★ ★

The 1954 Winner of the Trophy
Proposed by **Sir Alan Herbert**

Presentation to
Skipper Robert Williamson
by
Sir Alan Herbert

Reply by
Skipper Robert Williamson

★ ★

The Chairman
Proposed by **Mr. F. E. Catchpole**, O.B.E.
Reply by **The Chairman**

"What did the *Jessie Sinclair* catch?" I asked.

"Two hundred and seventy-two cran," Granda replied, "back in October; the first night of the competition."

That sounded a lot to me as four baskets were needed to make even one cran. They weren't the big baskets like the one Mam used to take clothes out to the line, but it was still a lot of fish.

I reached for *The Fishing News* and turned to the photo on the front page where Bob was shown accepting the trophy from a grey-haired man with glasses. Dad said his name was A.P. Herbert – Sir Alan Herbert the newspapers called him – and it was he who had made the presentation on behalf of Madame Prunier. Both Shetland papers carried a photo of this taking place, where I could see that he was tall like Dad.

Dad said he had made a good speech and had mentioned how big some members of the crew were compared to Bob. Giants, the papers said.

The next morning, we were all in the back having breakfast and Mam and Dad were telling us how they'd enjoyed the previous evening. They described how the hall was set out with rows of folding chairs and how they'd had to sit at the front.

"And the biggest fun," Mam said, "was when a peerie boy was reciting *Humpty Dumpty* and Dad's chair collapsed under him." We all laughed at that.

But I wasn't amused. No bairns, they'd said. It wasn't for bairns, they'd said.

I'd know better next time.

CHAPTER NINE

We visited Burra a lot, either for weekends or for longer breaks. During the summer holidays, when Dad was at the herring fishing, we spent a lot of time in Hamnavoe either with Auntie Jessie and Auntie Maggie who lived in my mother's old home, or at Granda's with him, Auntie Etta and our cousin Robert. Sometimes, Mam sent Robina and me to Burra on our own for a time before she joined us. When she was with us, Dad would join us at weekends.

Child's Play

It was a fine day, so after breakfast I decided to go and see what Marjory and Ann were up to. I walked along Duke Street, over the Clate Road and up the closs between Granda's and Lang Smithie's. This took me to an open grassy area with houses on three sides. It was here that Auntie Etta often hung washing beside an old quarry that was now little more than a dent in the landscape. Ahead of me the ground sloped gently to provide the well-trodden path to Auntie Tommy's, where Marjory and Ann lived. As I made my way up I was careful not to catch my foot in one of the two narrow drainage ditches that ran downhill and which were more difficult to spot now that the grass was growing again.

The girls weren't in.

"They're down at Bakkaburn," Auntie Tommy told me.

Bakkaburn was the small stony beach that lay in the shelter of Grola, a low headland at the head of the voe, not far from the Hamnavoe houses. I left by the front gate, skirted the quarry and set off down the slope and back across the Clate Road. As I passed the shed, where Marjory and Ann's father built boats with his brother Philip, I had a clear view of the beach where several peerie boats were drawn up. The tide was out and, right by the sea edge, I could see my cousins.

Below the shed, the slope was steeper, but I trod carefully and soon reached the Bakkaburn well, a rectangular structure of cement and stones with a large iron pump on top that stood a little way back from the beach. Even though the houses now had piped water, I had been to the well with Auntie Maggie when the tap water ran brown.

Hamnavoe in the 1950s. *Photo by C J Williamson, courtesy of Willie Smith*

Just then Ann turned round and called out to me so I stepped off the grass and made my way across the shingle to join her and her sister. In front of us a couple of paper boats were making uncertain headway from the shore. I picked up a small stone and joined my cousins in their efforts to drive the boats further. We did this by throwing stones gently into the water so as to create waves that would steer the boats away from us.

After a bit, we began aiming beyond the boats so that the force of the water drove the little craft back to shore. We repeated this a few times till the boats, being made of folded newspaper, became too waterlogged to float. It was time to find another game.

Searching for suitable stones with which to control the boats, we'd avoided choosing any that were too flat; those had another purpose altogether and we now sought them out. The first one I picked up was sandy-coloured and a few inches long. The side that lay uppermost in my hand had a slight roundness away from its edge, but the sea had smoothed all roughness from its surface. I turned it over. The underside was even better; though it did look as if a slice had at one time been chiselled away, what remained was almost perfectly level.

I stood up to my full height and looked around. My cousins had also been lucky in their searches and were standing a little way apart, close to the water's edge. Marjory went first; with her feet pointing towards the sea, and her precious stone held flat in her right hand, she twisted round to the right to draw her arm back before bringing it forward quickly to release the stone. It flew low over the water before dipping down to brush

With cousins Ann, left, and Marjory, right, at Bakkaburn.

the surface with just enough force to trigger the appearance of a ripple. As this disturbance resolved itself into a widening circle, the three of us concentrated on the stone, watching intently as it bounced up then dropped again to skim the surface a bit further on. This was repeated a few times till, losing momentum, the stone sank out of sight, leaving a trail of circles, misshapen now, in its wake.

It was Ann's turn next, then mine. I got myself into position and threw; the sandy-coloured stone was a good choice and it splashed its way through several leaps before it too disappeared. After a few more attempts each, we spread out to begin the hunt for a different shape of stone, more cylindrical this time.

Ann went first and, holding her stone upright in her hand, she threw it up, high over the water. From its highest point it dropped straight into the sea with a satisfying glug of a sound. 'Corking the bottle' we called it and finding suitable stones for this new activity kept us busy right across the beach.

We lost interest in this pursuit only when we found ourselves at the far side of Bakkaburn where the beach came to a sudden stop alongside a string of large boulders that nestled under the banks of Grola – the Staney Pier. This was smaller than the other Staney Pier that lay alongside the main Hamnavoe Pier; this pier's function was to provide a means of getting in and out of small boats that were light enough to manoeuvre this close to the shore. The rocks from which it had been constructed were of more or less equal height and smooth on top so as to give a reasonably flat walkway for anyone prepared to stride from one to the next.

Beside this pier, the Bakkaburn shingle gave way to an area where brown sand predominated and that claimed our attention. Unlike the large expanse of brilliant white sand permanently accessible at Meal, the Bakkaburn sand was often under water, but thanks to the ebbtide, its sandy surface now yielded a wealth of items crying out for further investigation: there were shells; little bits of seaweed, bright green or tawny-brown; sea-washed pieces of glass from broken bottles or jars that had lost their sharp edges and were now safe to pick up; and a scattering of pebbles, some half-buried.

With my fingers, I dug a flat stone out from the sand and skimmed it across the water. As it sank, I bent down to retrieve a piece of green glass that was partly submerged in a mixture of sand and gravel. It was roughly circular and had on it, raised markings of some kind. To see better what those were, I ventured to the sea edge, bent down and washed the glass. Once its gritty covering had been completely removed, I could tell that the markings were the remains of lettering, smudged now by the action of the sea. This was a prize worth keeping so I laid it carefully on the Staney Pier; it could stay there till it was time for me to go home.

Marjory and Ann had already climbed onto the pier and I now followed. We had to be careful as some of the rocks were under water at high tide, but it was the pools of water left behind that were the main attraction. I bent down at the first of those I came to. Limpets clung to the sides of the pool. I knew better than to try and remove them; they knew how to cling on. I stirred the water with my hand and a small crab scuttled along the bottom.

Just then a loud whistle was heard. We stopped what we were doing.

"Denner time," Marjory said.

"Is that your Mam?" I asked.

The girls shook their heads. "No, but it's a signal to someone."

Lots of mothers had whistles that they used to summon their offspring. I wasn't sure which was which, but knew that Auntie Etta had one to let Robert know it was time to come home. Then another whistle sounded. As most people ate at one o'clock it was a fair assumption that that time was near.

We made our way down from the pier. I picked up my piece of glass and we headed home; my cousins back to Westlea and me to Duke Street where Aunties Jessie and Maggie would soon have the denner on the table.

It had been a good morning.

CHAPTER TEN

Meal Picnic

"It can't be long now," Robina said.

It was a sunny day and we were sitting on the grass in front of the Duke Street house, looking out for the arrival of the *Tirrick*. The denner dishes had been cleared away so Auntie Jessie and Auntie Maggie were there too, on their usual seat below the ben window. Mam was alongside them, on the heavy wooden chair she'd carried out from the kitchen.

"Here she is," Auntie Jessie said, as the cross-shaped mast appeared in view beyond the Point.

"Mam," I said, scrambling up, "can we go and help with the kirns?"

"Off you go," she replied.

A quick glance at the voe showed that the *Tirrick* was already in full sight and heading for the pier. Robina and I ran along to the milk shop door where the large, lidded milk cans stood in an uneven cluster of different sizes. They were empty since Auntie Maggie had sold the milk this morning and it was now time for them to go back on the boat.

All but the smallest kirns had two handles, one on each side. Robina and I couldn't lift the largest of them, but we did find one we could manage between us, taking a lug each. By the time we'd made our selection, Andrew the boatman was by our side. He'd come to fetch the kirns but, as usual, was happy for us to help.

On the way down to the pier, we found ourselves in the company of passengers about to board the boat for its return trip to Scalloway. As they hurried purposefully on, we came face to face with others who'd just

Summer holiday in Burra.

arrived in Hamnavoe. We knew some of them, people who lived locally and were now hurrying home, but others, conversing in unfamiliar accents, wandered up the pier in a leisurely fashion, cameras at the ready. Tourists. Maybe Auntie Jessie and Auntie Maggie would be opening the tearoom this afternoon.

Uncle Hancie was waiting on board the *Tirrick* and soon took charge of the kirn, placing it on the open area of deck in front of the wheelhouse. By the time we'd delivered a second milk can to the boat, I noticed that some of the tourists were heading up the Muckle Road. No doubt, Uncle Hancie and Andrew had directed them to the sands by way of the Meal Kirk, the easiest route to explain to visitors.

When all the kirns had been dealt with, Robina and I went back to the house where we found Mam still sitting outside, but she was alone. Jessie and Maggie had obviously seen the tourists and begun their preparations. The tearoom was in the same building as the milk shop and also belonged to Uncle Hancie, but it was Auntie Jessie and Auntie Maggie who ran it for him.

"Mam," I said, "are you taking us to the sands this afternoon?" She'd said she would if it came a fine day.

She nodded and said, "It should be sheltered enough. Go and get ready."

We hurried indoors. All our stuff was ben where the three of us slept and we soon looked out our buckets and spades as well as our bathing costumes. We stripped off and got into our swimsuits, helping each other tie those at the neck before starting to put our clothes on again over the costumes. This would save time at the sands and we were struggling back into our summer dresses when Mam came in.

She'd helped herself to one of the deep leather-looking shopping bags that belonged to her sisters and now picked up her purse from the dressing table that stood across the corner in past the window.

"Are we having a picnic?" Robina asked.

"Would you like that?" Mam replied, while helping Robina fasten her Clark's sandals.

Once we were both fully dressed again, we followed Mam out of the house. A picnic meant a trip to Robbie's shop.

At the end of Duke Street, Mam made us look carefully to left and right in case there were vehicles about, but any that had gathered for the boat's arrival had long since dispersed. We crossed the Muckle Road and made our way across the Beach. Robina walked ahead of me, the tyals of her swimsuit sticking out at her back neck. I knew mine would be doing the same and made a half-hearted attempt to push them out of sight, but without much hope of success.

As we approached the shop, I said, "Can I ask?"

"Can I?" Robina said.

"Catherine, you ask for the lemonade; Robina the ..."

"Biscuits!"

"That's right," Mam said, as we went up the steps and into the shop. Robbie's sister Teenie was serving.

"Three peerie bottles of Mowat's Kola;" I said, "we're going to the sands."

"It'll be fine there today," Teenie replied, as she placed three small glass bottles on the counter.

"That's what Mam says," I said.

Robina stepped forward. "Custard creams." A perfect choice.

Back at the house, Mam fetched a bottle opener from the kitchen and placed it in the bag with our purchases, a towel, her makkin, and a

The Peerie Saands.

cardigan for each of us. Robina and I grabbed our buckets and spades, and we were off.

Instead of following the tourists up the Muckle Road, we went along to the other end of Duke Street and up the slope towards Granda's. I looked to see if Auntie Etta was in the garden, but there was no sign of life, so we kept going up the closs and straight ahead towards Auntie Tommy's. The end window of her kitchen was steamed up, but I thought I got a glimpse of someone moving about inside. However, Mam said we shouldn't stop and led us onto the Shelly Road, a path scattered with bits of broken yoag shell.

Soon we'd crossed the School Road, passed the school and were heading up the brae to Uncle Walter's, the last of the Hamnavoe houses. Auntie Mimie was in the front porch with her knitting.

"We're having a picnic," Robina told her, "at the sands."

"A good day for it," she replied, perfectly in tune with Mam and Teenie.

Behind Walter and Mimie's house the land sloped away from us in a steep incline of uneven ground covered in tufts of rough grass. Mam took Robina's hand while I went ahead clinging on fiercely to my bucket and spade as my feet negotiated a way downhill to where a wire fence ran across our path.

The slope was barely noticeable now; the ground almost, but not quite, level. To make it easier to cross the fence, someone had removed the upper strands of wire and placed a large flat stone underneath for standing on. Despite those refinements, I knew from last year's trips to the sands that keeping my balance before stepping down again from this improvised step was tricky. I needed something to hold on to, but the nearest fencepost, lacking its full complement of wire, stood at such an angle that it didn't promise much by way of support. Best to wait for Mam.

It didn't take Mam and Robina long to catch up with me and, with Mam's help, we were soon on our way, making good progress over sheep-cropped grass. The sheep and their lambs, large now, kept out of our way as we reached a planticrub, a circle of stone covered in greyish-green lichen with traces of sheep's wool. I stood on tiptoe to try and see what was inside, but all I got was a glimpse of huge rhubarb leaves.

After a bit, we reached the rigs where vegetables and other crops were planted. From here we could see the far end of the Meal Saands. Glaringly white in the sunshine, the sands were under repeated attack from blue-green waves that rushed ashore then flattened out into white foam.

"Mam," I asked, "are we going to the big sands?"

"No," she said, "we'll just go to the Peerie Saands today."

Those lay in a geo, not far from the other side of the rigs, but first, we had to get across and the only way to do that was by a narrow strip of grass, just a few inches wide, that had been left to grow in between the rows of plants.

I went first, arms out from my sides, bucket and spade dangling uncertainly over the crops as I tried to keep my feet on the meagre pathway. Once across, I looked round. Robina had started following me, but I noticed that Mam had taken charge of her bucket and spade. Rather than tackle the climb down into the Peerie Saands on my own, I wandered over to a nearby stile from where I had a good view over the whole length of the big sands. Some family groups had already taken up position well back from the sea edge and I noticed that the tourists were making their way down the grassy slope from the Meal Kirk.

When Robina and Mam were safely across the rigs, Mam called me over to the Peerie Saands. White as their neighbour, the sands were surrounded by rocks that rose to form a cliff face part of the way round.

However, in front of where Mam and Robina now waited, was a gentler slope. Grass-covered at first, this incline gave way to sloping black rocks that provided a way down to the sands.

"Now, help your sister," Mam said, as I started making my way down.

I stopped and held out my hand, but Robina needed very little help and soon we were on the sandy floor. Mam found a comfortable seat on the warm rocks and got out her knitting while Robina and I stripped to our bathing costumes and ran towards the water.

The waves that rolled onto the sand here were less fierce than those at the big sands, but behaved in much the same way, flattening out into foam as they ran up the beach, and this was where we tested the water with our toes. This far up, it wasn't too cold and I stood still, facing out to sea, as the water was sucked out again. In front of me, meandering paths of clear water formed while my feet slowly sank into the shiny smooth sand left behind.

I enjoyed this experience a few more times before moving a good bit further down the beach where Robina joined me and we braced ourselves for the sea's return. The drenching we got at the force of the waves was cold, but we were exhilarated, splashing each other excitedly before running back up to fetch our buckets and spades. Time to think about a sandcastle.

We picked a spot, far enough from the sea edge not to be disturbed by the waves, knelt down and began to dig. The damp sand that lay under the dry surface was perfect for building and we soon had the basic structure, long, narrow, and flat on top. Robina wandered off looking for something to use as decoration.

I filled my bucket with sand, pressing it down till I was sure it would take no more, then cautiously upended it on top of the castle. I held my breath as it came out cleanly enough and stayed in place for a second or two, but then a crack appeared in its smooth surface and a section slid from the whole in a messy heap. I was sweeping away the debris with my hand when I noticed that Mam was watching.

"Try again," she said.

The next attempt was successful and I was trying to create a matching turret at the other end when Robina returned with some bits of shell, spoot among them, a couple of small sea-washed stones and odd bits of dried grass. Another turret finally in place and the decoration completed, I looked over to Mam. She'd put away her makkin and had got out the towel.

"Go and wash the sand off your hands," she called out.

We didn't need a second telling and were soon back with her as she dried our hands and arms and tried to remove as much sand from our backs and legs as one small towel could cope with.

We sat down on the sand in front of Mam as she opened a bottle of kola each then held out the opened packet of custard creams. This wasn't like the picnic in my Mickey Mouse book with a tablecloth and cakes and plates and cutlery, but it did taste good. The kola finished and the packet of biscuits depleted, it was time to return to Duke Street.

Mam helped us out of our costumes and into our clothes, encouraging us to put on our cardigans for the walk back. Before crossing the rigs again, I had one last look at the big sands where I noticed that the tourists were also leaving. They'd be going to the tearoom.

There would be no kola there.

CHAPTER ELEVEN

After primary two, I was put into Miss Wishart's class in the main school building and was still with her in primary four when Robina began school, but after Christmas, during Robina's second term, the infant class was moved from the school to Scalloway Public Hall. This chapter begins a few weeks later.

The Hall School

When I got home from school, Mam was running water into the kitchen sink. On the draining board beside her, lay several large haddocks on a string. I went over for a closer look.

"Don't get your school clothes in a mess," she said.

"I've got a letter for you," I replied, "from the Maister. He came in with them this afternoon. He was wearing his glasses."

As Mam rinsed her hands and turned off the tap, I moved back from the sink, opened my schoolbag and took out a small envelope.

"We all got them," I added, handing it over.

The note she removed was short. After she'd glanced quickly at it, she put it in her apron pocket and turned towards the sink, to get on with cleaning the fish for our tea.

"What is it?" I asked. "They didn't tell us."

"Go and get out of your school clothes first," she said.

By the time I got back, the fish were gutted and skinned and lying on a floury plate. Mam was at the cooker, cutting chunks of cooking fat into the big black frying pan. I watched as the pieces hit the hot surface, were still for a moment then moved off, leaving shiny polished trails.

Mam would be too busy to speak to me when she put the fish in, so I asked again,

"What is it, in the letter?"

"You've to go to the hall next week," she said, "the public hall."

"Oh, that," I said, "I know, the school's too small."

P4 and P5 at Scalloway Public Hall. *Back:* Jimmy Watt, Bertie Burgess, Frank Gilfillan, John Alex Johnson, Sydney Goodlad, Tommy Watt, Cecil Goudie, Walter Abernethy, Alex Johnson, Brian Watt. *Middle:* Drew Sutherland, Laurence Wishart, Margaret Watt, Rena Fraser, Margaret Smith, Margaret Upson, Martin Jamieson, Frank Johnson, Kenneth Gifford, Alan Young. *Front:* Margaret Gilbertson, Mary Thomson, Morvyn Watt, Marie Georgeson, Iris Morrison, Vivian Sinclair, the author, Christine Tait, Linda Goodlad.

Photo by Eddie Sinclair

The earlier decision to send infants to the hall had not been popular with parents so, after only a few weeks, primaries one and two were returning to the school.

Just last month our Sunday School Christmas party had taken place in the hall, but most of the events there, whether concerts, dances, weddings, sales, SWRI meetings, whist drives or film shows, were predominantly for adults. It might be quite exciting to claim it as our own.

"Your father and I still don't like it," Mam broke into my thoughts.

"But it's nearer," I interrupted. "I won't get wet going to school." The hall wasn't far from the house; we could see it from the back windows. "We're to be in the peerie hall," I went on, "Mrs Sutherland will be there as well, with primary five."

"Her class will be upstairs," Mam said.

"Oh," I said, intrigued. I'd seen the stairs, but I'd never seen anyone use them. The heavy wooden gate across the bottom of the stairway was always locked. Maybe lessons in the hall would afford me the opportunity to explore further.

Come Monday morning, I was ready in good time and soon on my way, keen to experience a different kind of classroom. Robina hadn't said much about her few weeks in the hall and, despite the longer walk involved, seemed happy enough to be returning to the school building. As she headed up the road, I turned in the opposite direction. I rounded the post box corner to follow Houl Road past the top of Chapel Lane and on, till I faced an open area of roadway in front of the hall where several streets met. Overlooking this intersection was the hall itself, standing in a raised position between Gibblestone Road and Berry Road.

Several pupils ahead of me were making their way across the junction, but I hesitated as a car was approaching up Burnet's Closs from the direction of the Street. It turned right and disappeared round the other side of the hall.

As I stepped off the pavement, it struck me that the hall didn't provide us with much of a playground. I should have asked Robina where the infants played during their time at the hall.

A wall, topped by wrought iron railings, curved round the front of the building and all the way back to enclose an area of grass and trees on the Berry Road side, but clearly that wasn't a big enough area for us all to run around in. I knew there was a piece of waste ground behind the hall, but that wouldn't be suitable either and, on the Gibblestone Road side, much of the space that had existed was taken up by an extension to the hall. It was hardly likely that the teachers would send us out to play in the street. I'd have to wait till playtime to see what the arrangements were.

I entered the hall grounds by way of a set of high wrought iron gates. The gates matched the railings, but close up, it was difficult not to notice how the paint had begun blistering and peeling, giving way to rust. The gates stood open and, once inside, I bounded up a flight of stone steps and headed round the side of the hall, drawn by the excited clamour of pupils.

Those who'd arrived first were crowded onto the steps of the main entrance, two heavy wooden doors set into the wall of a tower constructed on the Berry Road side of the hall. I found a spot on the bottom step and joined in the speculation as to whether or not the teachers had arrived, but the small panes of bullseye glass in the top section of the doors yielded no secrets.

Eventually those at the top of the steps reported signs of movement and the right hand side of the door was pushed open and secured to the outside wall by a brass hook. A handbell was rung and, after a momentary hesitation, we surged forward into the entrance hall.

"My class to the stairs," said Mrs Sutherland. I couldn't resist an upward glance into the mysterious stairwell, taking in as I did so, the fact that the wooden gate had been removed and set to the side.

Meanwhile, opposite the foot of the stairs, Miss Wishart was opening one side of a set of high double doors whose top halves were heavy with panes of glass on which hung generous amounts of black cloth. I'd assumed we were on our way to the cloakrooms where we'd left our coats during the Sunday School party, but instead Miss Wishart brought us to a halt as soon as we stepped through the doors.

We were in a gloomy inner vestibule: a part of the hall we'd usually pass through without pause. On our right was a set of doors identical to those we'd just come through, also blacked out, so that the glass did nothing to relieve the murkiness of where we now found ourselves. A feeling of surprise hung in the air. We knew this second set of doors led directly into the main hall and that was where the cloakrooms were to be found, in behind the stage, one for boys and the other for the girls.

The only light in this unfamiliar place was from a single electric bulb suspended within a discoloured shade and, in its indifferent glow, I became aware of bare floorboards and walls of dark varnished wood. This dim dusty place might not be somewhere we'd usually be found loitering, but the school had found a purpose for it.

"Coats are to be hung up here," Miss Wishart said, indicating black metal pegs that had been fixed at child height in one of the dark walls.

As she spoke, she opened one of two smaller doors leading off the vestibule to give us our first glimpse into the peerie hall in its new guise. Facing us, our desks stood in rows, not singly, but in pairs, just as they had been in our classroom in the school.

Our coats hung up, we entered our new classroom. To the right of the door, propped up on a sturdy wooden easel, stood a large blackboard, its surface streaked with white where the duster had failed to remove all traces of chalk. As I wondered where my desk was, I spotted to the left of the door, a school cupboard and, alongside it, Miss Wishart's desk, still a familiar sight even though it was almost hidden under piles of books and jotters. A large map of Scotland, traced out on what looked to me like a giant sheet of brown wrapping paper, was pinned to one wall.

However, despite these modifications, the original purpose of this square-shaped space was still in evidence. Behind the teacher's desk was a door that I knew led to the hall kitchen, and the apparently solid wooden wall on which the map was displayed was, in fact, the heavy movable partition that I'd often seen folded back to provide extra seating space for the main hall beyond.

Miss Wishart asked my class to wait while she directed primary three, two at a time, to the seats closest to the partition. The act of sitting down had a calming effect on the younger children and, once they were settled, Miss Wishart turned to us.

She began by asking Vivian and me to sit at the two desks in the back corner of what was clearly going to be the primary four side of the room. As we took our seats, I realised that I hadn't got my old desk. This one had a small drawing etched into it: a hull, two triangular sails and the start of a line underneath that might have been intended as sea. Had the artist been apprehended by Miss Wishart, mid-scribble?

I lifted the lid, but the desk was empty. Miss Wishart had taken in all our school books last week so I replaced the lid and sat back. As the last members of my class took their appointed seats, the buzz that had accompanied us in from the front door gave way to an air of expectancy.

Miss Wishart's response was to pick up a pile of jotters from her table and take them over to primary three, where youngsters in the front seats helped by passing them back through the rows. In their anonymous blue covers it was hard to work out which jotters these were: English, Handwriting or something else. When Miss Wishart turned her attention to my class and I saw the pupils in front of us open jotters ruled in squares, I had the answer: Sums.

Next came our Holmes McDougall text books; thin and floppy, and lightly disguised by the paper covers we'd been required to provide. Mine were of brown wrapping paper, carefully cut and folded to fit by Dad who'd written the name of the book, *Comprehensive Arithmetic*, as well as my own, and my class, neatly on the front.

Miss Wishart told us which exercise to turn to. It was one we'd begun last week and she now wanted us to find it. It was hard to concentrate in these new surroundings and my mind soon wandered. Miss Wishart hadn't mentioned playtime. Where would we go? The main hall was just through the partition; would we have to play there and not get out at all?

When I did manage to finish my sums, I took my jotter out to Miss Wishart's desk. Her desk wasn't like our ones; it was more like a table, but with drawers along the side where Miss Wishart sat. She was there now, a line of children to her left. I joined this queue and waited to get my work marked.

However, before I could be seen, Miss Wishart stood up, turned round, opened the door to the kitchen and disappeared inside. Usually we stood quietly, but this was something new.

"She's gone to put on the kettle," someone half-whispered.

"It must be playtime," someone else said. When Miss Wishart returned, she asked us to go back to our seats, opened the cupboard door and took out a handbell. A murmur ran round the class and the children still at their desks put down their pencils.

"At playtime," she said, "you're allowed to play in the park."

She meant the Fraser Park which had its main entrance from the Street, but there was also a small gate across from the hall. Miss Wishart went on to tell us we had to stay close to the gate and not cross the football pitch, but there would be no reason to anyway, as the swings, seesaws and roundabout were all chained up for the winter.

This was good news: first we'd got the hall to ourselves, and now the park. Our parents might not be too happy, but I was going to enjoy these new arrangements.

CHAPTER TWELVE

Picture Perfect

Lessons over for the day, we hurried out of the room: it was Thursday and there would be films in the hall at night. I struggled into my coat as quickly as I could and picked up the little brown case that served as a schoolbag before joining Vivian, who had reached for the brass handle on one of the double doors of our makeshift cloakroom. Together, we began to push at the lower part of the heavy door, ignoring as best we could, the threads and torn strips of material from the blackout fabric that hung down to tickle our faces. As the door responded, we stepped into the welcome brightness of the outer hallway.

On the way towards the main door, Vivian asked, "Are you going to the pictures tonight?"

"Are you?" I replied, guessing that she might be. "Don't know if Mam'll let me," I added.

"Why not?" The daylight that had been so welcome a minute before, now allowed me to see Vivian's expression and she looked as if any parental opposition were my fault.

"Dunno," I shrugged, "she doesn't like the hall."

"The hall," Vivian looked back, "but it's where you go to school."

"Yes, and she doesn't think much of that either."

None of the parents did, but that didn't prevent them allowing their offspring to attend films.

"What's on tonight?" I asked, not entirely certain I wanted to know.

"Not sure," Vivian replied, "but we can find out."

So, instead of heading home, Vivian and I crossed the roadway in front of the hall and set off down Burnet's Closs. There was no pavement and, at first, nothing to see except high walls on either side, but the lane was little more than a hundred yards long and we soon arrived at the junction with Main Street. On our left stood Spencie's hotel, but our interest lay in the side window of the chemist shop to the right where the usual typed notice from the Highlands and Islands Film Guild was on display. We studied it carefully; along with date, time and place, it gave us the title, *Doctor in the House*.

"What's that about?" I asked, but Vivian didn't know either.

"Do you think you'll be able to go?" she asked.

I couldn't tell. Mam's decisions about films seemed pretty arbitrary to me,

"I'll tell her what it's called," I said, checking the notice once more. "*Doctor - in - the - House.*" I repeated the title slowly, to fix it in my mind.

With that, we turned to walk back up the way we'd come. Ahead of us was the hall with its clock tower on top. It was only a few minutes since the bell had rung, but I was expected straight home at the end of the school day. Surely Mam wouldn't object to such a short detour. Would she? Besides, she'd definitely not let me go if I couldn't provide at least a name for the film.

At teatime, the usual battle took place. The Film Guild brought films to the hall every second Thursday at 7.30, doors open at 7.00. Everyone knew that, but my mother treated each request for the entrance money as if films were something new and alien.

"The pictures," she said. "What's on? What's it about?" Pointless to say that, if she really wanted an answer to her second question, she'd have to let me see the film first.

Instead, I said, "Vivian's going."

Mam was unmoved.

"When's Dad coming home?" I asked.

"He's not," Mam said, "they're going in to Voe."

That happened sometimes when they were fishing up north in the winter, but on this occasion, it also deprived me of an opportunity to try for a more favourable decision from Dad.

"He'd let me go," I said.

"Do you think so?" Mam laughed. "What was it called again?"

I told her, more hopeful now that I wasn't getting a downright refusal and, sure enough, by the time the dishes were cleared away, she'd got her purse from the kitchen cabinet and handed me the cost of admission to the films.

I took the money, wondering, and not for the first time, if this were some elaborate game Mam played for which I must not be told the rules.

I arrived at the hall just as the doors were opening and followed the crowd inside and across the entrance hall to the first of the double doors. Here, movement slowed almost to a standstill as formless groupings of people became a queue waiting to gain entrance through the next set of doors. This meant passing through the inner vestibule with its new coat pegs – a dark cheerless space that had assumed a new significance, except no-one else seemed to notice.

Soon it was my turn to hand over my entrance money to the man at the table just inside the main hall. As well as a box for the money, he had rolls of tickets in front of him and tore one off for me. I put it in my pocket.

The hall was dimly lit, the windows blacked out and only some of the lights switched on, but there was more than enough light for me to find my way past the rows of bentwood chairs to the wooden forms at the front where several children were already seated.

Vivian saw me arrive. "You've managed to get here," she said.

I nodded and found a space to sit among our classmates. There was a great deal of excited chatter – and not all from the children. I looked round to take in a good-sized audience of older schoolchildren and grown-ups seated on the chairs behind us.

The ticket seller was still busy at the door and the hall-keeper, Willie Lowrie, was nearby greeting audience members as they made their way in. In the centre aisle, Geordie Horne from the Film Guild was by the projector where it stood facing the screen at the front.

I turned to face the front again. There being nothing to see on the screen, I tilted my head right back and turned my gaze to the space above our heads. There was no ceiling, but I could make out the underside of the roof as it sloped upwards from either side of the hall to form a peak so high that I could barely make it out. It was lined with varnished wood and held in place by carved wooden rafters. I liked this mysterious construction and found it imposing and appropriate for such an important building, but my mother said the high roof made the hall cold and that gave her one more excuse to try and keep me at home when I wanted to go to the pictures.

Someone walked past the end of our row; it was Willie Lowrie on his way to switch off the lights. He went up steps beside the stage and disappeared through the door at the top. The noise in the hall died down to an expectant hush before Willie reappeared and, with a torch to guide him, made his way once again towards the back of the hall. The screen flickered and came to life with a countdown of numbers, then a title screen and the first part of the programme began. We had a cartoon first then the familiar crowing cock that signalled Pathé News.

Eventually the main feature began. It was very funny. There were several students who were training to be doctors except Kenneth More who didn't want to pass his exams as he'd then lose the money someone was giving him to study. There was an old surgeon, the demanding Lancelot Sprat. Sprat was played by James Robertson Justice who always made us laugh, but best of all, Dirk Bogarde was in it. I liked Dirk Bogarde. He reminded me of pictures I'd seen of Robert Burns and I wished they'd make a film in which he could play the poet.

When I got home, I sat on the stool by the fire with my shoes off and my feet on the warm hearth.

Mam soon had the kettle boiling and produced a cup of Horlicks. "This'll warm you up," she said, "then it's off to bed."

"It was a good film," I said, "Dirk Bogarde was in it. It was a comedy," but Mam was more interested in making sure I had a good night's sleep.

During playtime the next day, someone asked in the manner of James Robertson Justice, "What's the bleeding time?"

"It's ten past ten," the rest of us responded amidst uproarious laughter.

Just then the bell rang. "No it's not," some spoilsport said, "it's time to get back."

"What's the next film?" I asked Vivian, as we traipsed once more into the hall.

CHAPTER THIRTEEN

Fetching the Errands

"Catherine," I heard my mother call from the kitchen, "put that book down, will you."

"Coming," I replied, inserting one arm half-heartedly into the sleeve of my coat.

My attention though, was still on the Secret Seven adventure that bobbed up and down in my other hand. As I struggled with the coat, the movement made it difficult for me to focus on the print. Just then, Mam appeared in the living room doorway; she was holding my knitted bonnet.

"The sooner you go ..." she began.

"All right," I replied, swapping the book to my other hand.

"You can't put your coat on like that," she added, "give me the book."

I sighed and put the book down on the stool by the fire. When I'd got the coat on properly, Mam helped me with the bonnet. I tilted my head backwards and she fastened it under my chin. I followed her into the kitchen where she gave me her large black shopping bag along with the small leather purse from the dresser.

"There's a line," she said, "for Andy the butcher's and Mowat's."

It was the Easter holidays and the weather was damp and blustery. A fresh breeze was in my face as I set off down the road. As I rounded the chapel corner, Mam's bag began to flap about in my hand. I held on firmly to its stout handles, fearful in case it filled with air and became a balloon that carried me off, like Winnie the Pooh in the story Miss Wishart read to us at school. This made me think of the book I'd been forced to abandon. What did Mam have against reading? She preferred knitting, for some reason.

Clinging tightly to the shopping bag, I approached Main Street which ran roughly east to west, following the curve of the shoreline. There were very few buildings on the lower side of the roadway, making it open to sea breezes for much of its length.

I joined the Street half-way along, at the Co-op corner from where I had an uninterrupted view of the voe. The water was dark and choppy, the air above blurred by a fine mist of spray. Head down, I set off along the uneven pavement, past shops, Spencie's hotel, the banks and the entrance to the Fraser Park.

At Mowat's there was some shelter from the draper's shop opposite. One of Mowat's bakers was standing by the open door of the bakehouse, his white cap and apron, shirt and grey trousers, all dusted with flour. Only his red face provided a splash of colour. He spoke to me. I said hello and pushed on. I'd call in at Mowat's shop on the way back.

The butcher's was at the east end of the Street; two large windows with a doorway in between. There was no sign, unless you counted the traces of sawdust deposited by departing feet on the uneven floor of the entrance. Through the glass of the inner door, I saw that the shop was busy, most of the customers being women in winter coats and woollen headsquares. I went in and squeezed past those nearest the door, into the corner where Andy had shelves of muddy potatoes, neeps, cabbages, carrots and onions. Most of the potatoes were made up in quarter-stone and half-stone bags, but the other vegetables were loose and strong-smelling.

You were expected to know whose turn it was, so I had a good look round, taking in who was ahead of me. There was much chat among the adults. Captain Hunter's wife, whose daughter did a bit of amateur acting, was leading the discussion on Thursday night's film in the hall.

Andy appeared from the back shop wearing his usual brown shop coat and stripy blue apron. He approached the counter and put something on the scales, probably mince. I saw him remove the red carpenter's pencil from behind his ear to add up what was owed.

I heard the next customer ask for frying steak. Andy picked up his large knife and walked round to where several sides of beef hung heavily on large metal hooks. The first carcase swung ominously from his attempted grasp. He steadied it and sliced through the fatty covering to the deep red meat inside. He cut what was required, returned to the counter and

Robina and me. *Photo by C J Williamson, courtesy of Willie Smith*

slapped the beef onto the scales. He adjusted the brass weights and told the customer the price.

Before it was my turn, I helped myself to a quarter-stone of potatoes. The brown paper bag had been twisted shut at the top, but was beginning to tear with the weight, so I had to nurse it carefully until it was my turn.

"A pound of sassermaet," I read from Mam's line.

He fetched some and dropped the marled red meat onto the scales. I watched the needle swing round. With his fingers, he removed some to get the weight right. He wrapped the meat in greaseproof paper and put it in a small brown bag before placing it on the counter, beside the potatoes.

"That's all," I said.

He told me how much it came to and I opened the flap on the black purse. When he'd handed over my change he helped me get my purchases into the shopping bag.

I had to be careful that the now heavy bag didn't drag on the ground as I made my way back to Mowat's. From the outside, Mowat's wasn't unlike the butcher's, except for the fancy gold lettering, *Mowat & Co*, over the doorway. I stepped into the small entrance and clicked open the brass catch of the inner door. As soon as I stepped inside, I could smell the bread.

I twisted round to look up at the old clock on the wall by the door. It had a huge white face with large Roman numerals round the edge. If you watched the heavy black hands carefully enough, you could see them move. Underneath, behind its own little glass window, the pendulum swung in time with the loud ticking that was always audible, however busy the shop should be. It was a few minutes after eleven: the time the new loaves were ready. You could buy cookies and fancies and groceries earlier, but I was here for a loaf.

I wasn't the only one. Most of the customers from Andy's seemed to be here, but I knew this would be a shorter wait. Mowat's sold more things than the butcher's did and Bob Mowat had several assistants. One of them, Mootie, was operating the bacon machine at one end of the counter and Jessie was busy with what Mam called "loose" butter, a large yellow block that had its own glass case on a shelf behind the counter. When the women had time, they used a big knife to make up pounds and half-pounds of butter that were wrapped in greaseproof paper and left inside the case, but the last lot had gone and Jessie was having to prepare some more for her customer.

The other assistant, Thelma, was over in the corner among the teabread and fancies. These were on shelves in a little compartment of their own that could only be reached from behind the counter. Customers were able to see the bread and cakes through a large glass window that stretched from counter height to the ceiling and this partition was right next to where I was standing, so I moved aside as Thelma's customer came over, pointing and calling, "Three muffins, three cookies ... and four coffee buns ... and four of those fancies with the pink icing."

I moved nearer to the counter and that gave me a good view of what Mootie was doing. She was serving the cook off a fishing boat. I didn't know him, but I'd seen fishermen buy their stores before. Mootie wrote down his purchases in a little book that had blue carbon paper sticking out round the edge: a huge amount of bacon, four loaves, lots of butter and bags of bakers' biscuits. She put the items in a strong box she'd fetched from the backshop before tying it up with sisal twine.

When she'd finished with him, she turned to me. "Yes, Catherine," she said.

I got out Mam's line; "a half loaf" it said.

"A ...," I hesitated, "a loaf," I said, not entirely confident that a loaf was a half loaf, even though that's what Mam said.

Why did mothers have to be so difficult? Who in their right mind could prefer makkin to reading and now she wanted me to ask for what sounded like half a loaf? Maybe I should just have given Mootie the purse, the way I used to do, before I could read.

Mootie returned with the new loaf. It was a beautiful snowy white, with little bits hanging off the sides where it had been pulled from the one baked next to it. She reached for a sheet of tissue paper and wrapped it deftly round the bread, finishing off with string, being careful not to tie the soft bread too tightly. She didn't cut the string, but did that trick where you wrap it round itself, and over your finger, then tug so the string breaks.

I paid for the loaf, left the shop and was soon on my way home. It was still breezy, with large raindrops in the wind. Oh, no. If I got wet Mam would make such a fuss. I hadn't had bronchitis since I was five, but she seemed to expect a recurrence with every shower.

Fortunately I got home reasonably dry, but by the time we'd had our denner, rain was lashing against the windows, driven by the squall. There'd be no going out to play this afternoon.

CHAPTER FOURTEEN

Mad March Days

(Cargoes, John Masefield)

I found Dad kneeling on the grass in his dungarees using his pliers with the red handles to remove wire from the fence behind our house. The fence, which separated our back green from that of the other house in our block, ran a long way back, right up to where it met the Gibblestone Road back greens.

"Why are you doing that?" I asked.

"Your mother wants a hedge. Some shelter from the south wind," he replied.

"Are you taking out all the wire, right along to the end?"

"No," he said, "just to where the long grass starts."

Mam and Dad had agreed not to cut a sizeable area of the grass that was closest to the Gibblestone Road houses. Archie Nicolson lived in one of those houses and the idea was to provide hay for his sheep.

"What about the fence posts?" was my next question.

"We'll leave them, and the hedge will cover them, the same as should happen over there." He nodded towards the flowering currant shrubs that had been planted in a line between us and our neighbours on the other side. I scuttled off for a closer look.

The layout was different at this side as the houses weren't joined together so the hedge began right up at the front garden wall. I paused at a point opposite our back door where a gap had been left in the planting that would allow Mam and Lizzie May to visit each other unhindered.

Beyond the gap, the shrubs continued to where our sheds were built close to the fence on either side.

After the starkness of winter, a faint greenness now hung round the thin branches. I reached out to touch the bright green tips of leaves emerging from the buds of winter and wondered when they'd be abundant enough to disguise the fence posts.

The weather then took a turn for the worse. A fierce southerly gale like the one Mam had in mind when she decided on the new hedge, swept in off the sea.

"Make sure you keep your hood up on the way to school," Mam said. "We don't want you getting ill again."

"I've just got to get as far as the hall," I replied.

Mam was silent. She was unhappy that some classes had had to be transferred to the Scalloway hall and was unlikely therefore to acknowledge any advantage to the arrangement.

"Mind," she repeated, "keep your hood up."

On the way to the hall, I caught sight of the voe, a stage set for a dismal day. The sky was a distant backdrop of heavy grey, patched with black. Downstage hung misty cloud, a giant curtain caught in a draught that allowed us glimpses only, of the landscape. Across this scene, sheets of rain were being driven inland, mingling with salt spray as the wind whipped up even the waters of the sheltered voe. The angry blast then attacked the village, gusting in all directions as it bounced off buildings and collided with itself in its efforts to disrupt.

Concentration on schoolwork was difficult. "Four sixes are ... twenty- ... five ... no, twenty-four. Down the two ... no, down the five ... four. Twenty-four ... down the four and carry the two." The next figure was a seven. "How can anyone multiply a seven in this?"

I put my pencil down and looked towards the high windows of the peerie hall where the swirling wind was casting regular bursts of water onto the outside of the glass. The currents of wet running down the panes left salty smears that further darkened the gloomy room.

It was too wild for us to be allowed out at playtime. As the storm raged, we played in the main hall, our spirits high in response to both the squall outside and the fact of our incarceration. We chased one another up and down, swinging round wildly when a change of direction was indicated. No-one was "It". Like the unruly elements outside, our only rule was that there were no rules till the bell called us back to our desks.

By the end of the school day, the rain had gone off, but it took a great effort to keep our feet in the wind. We stood in the road, leaning slightly into the gale, our faces scrunched up taking its full force. With our schoolbags flapping energetically in our hands, we grasped our coat tails from behind and held them aloft to catch the gusts as we sailed along, a street full of small ships. With much exaggerated staggering and barging into one another, we headed home.

"Mam, do you have an old apron?" I asked, as I burst into the kitchen via the back door.

"What for?"

What for indeed, was she not aware of the weather? Adults really were hopeless at questions.

"For a parachute of course," I replied, "can I look in the bag?"

I had already opened the narrow broom cupboard beside the cooker. The sweet aroma of wax polish met me. In the bottom were the carpet sweeper, some sort of floor polishing gadget Mam had bought from a door-to-door salesman, and a large floor brush. Hanging up by its bamboo handle was a duster of dark brown feathers. Overhead and out of my reach on a high shelf were the more usual cloth dusters, some polishes and a bag of rags. This bag she reached down for me.

"Will this do?" she asked, picking out the remains of a dark wraparound flower-sprigged apron.

"Yes," I said, "have you got any string?"

She appeared not to have heard. "You can't go out to play in your school clothes."

By the time I had changed, she had found the string and was using scissors to cut out the largest possible square from the cloth. I helped her tie a piece of string to each corner and watched as she tied the four strings together with a much longer piece that would be used to fly the parachute.

In the back garden, holding tightly to the free end of the string, I threw the parachute up. It flapped about wildly, the strings twisting around one another. I pulled it in, untangled the mess and tried again. Eventually it caught the wind cleanly, the strings went taut and soon the dark square of precious material was billowing at the full extent of its line. There was quite a tug on the string. I moved up and down the back green enjoying the tussle. Exhilarated, I pretended it was going to sweep me upwards, but glanced towards the kitchen window for reassurance.

Mad March Days.   *Photo by W Williamson, courtesy of Elizabeth Marshall*

My mother was there and she was pointing to my right. Robina had appeared, also with a parachute, but a smaller one. She seemed to know what to do so I let her get on with it.

I moved away to avoid the two sets of lines getting tangled and found myself beside one of the three clothes poles. This gave me an idea and I began weaving in and out round the poles. Robina joined in. As our confidence grew, we moved more and more quickly, but had to work hard to keep our feet as well as control our parachutes.

Mam rapped hard on the window. "Teatime," she mouthed.

The wind was too noisy for us to hear her, but we went in anyway.

The next stage should have been the planting of the hedge, but a few days later something quite different had sprouted behind the house. No-one had told Robina or me to expect it. Before school, the coal box, the herring barrel and the clothes props were on their own below the kitchen window at the back of the house. After school, we could hardly get near them for an enormous long wooden object. It lay on the ground, like a felled telegraph pole, round, smooth and painted a sort of washed-out colour that would have been useful in paint boxes for people's faces. It was not of uniform thickness, but tapered towards one end. Propped up against the wall behind it, was a much shorter wooden arrangement, smooth as the longer section and painted the same colour, but fashioned in a pincer shape, like an elongated lobster with a single claw.

"Where did this come from?"

"What is it?"

"Why is it here?"

"It's a spar from the boat," we were told.

A few days later, Dad resumed work on the fence. I expected to find him removing more wire, but it was the fence posts mid-way along where the hedge would go that had his attention.

"What are you doing?" I demanded. "I thought they were going to be covered when the new hedge grows."

Dad half-smiled, half-shook his head and got on with his task. He was wearing dungarees again and, with a hammer and some bits of wood, was constructing brackets on top of each four neighbouring fence posts. Later the heavy spar was laid across the tops of the posts and lashed to these new supports.

All thoughts of shelter gone and hedge planting postponed, we soon claimed the spar as our own. Sitting on top of it, it was a car, a horse, a carriage, an aeroplane. Standing beside it, it became a counter, a barrier, a customs post or a barre like those in the ballet stories in our comics. Best of all, it was a stout climbing frame. In our more adventurous moments we hung underneath it, holding on by hands and knees, our heads thrown back so we could examine our surroundings from a different angle.

CHAPTER FIFTEEN

A Good Day

I dragged my feet on the gravelly ground, bringing the swing to a halt.

"Denner time," I called out to Robina.

We were on the swings in the Fraser Park so had a good view of the clock on top of the Scalloway Hall. I stood up and went to get my bike from where it lay on the grass. Robina joined me and we set off, walking with our bikes across the football pitch and up the banking in the direction of the top gate. I went first, half-carrying and half-pushing my bike up the steps to the gate itself and out onto the rough ground across from the hall.

We got on the bikes and cycled up Houl Road as far as the post box corner then turned into Meadowfield Road. As we passed the peerie shop, I noticed it was still open, so it couldn't be quite one o'clock yet. This gave us time to return our bikes to the shed before going in.

In the kitchen, the table was laid for denner and Mam was pouring the tatties at the sink. The small top section of window above her head was open, but traces of steam persisted on the larger pane below. Over on the cooker, the big soup pot simmered on a back plate while, on the dresser alongside, stood Mam's baking bowl, full of something wrapped in a dish towel: bannocks.

"Can I have a bannock?" I asked.

"Not just now," she said, "you know the bannocks are for tomorrow."

She was right; I did. Tomorrow would be the first Thursday in August – Scalloway regatta day.

"It's going to be a fine day," Mam said, when she came in to waken us the next morning.

"Who's coming today?" I asked.

"In this weather, I expect quite a few," she replied, pulling open the curtains before telling us which summer dresses and ankle socks she wanted us to wear.

When we got downstairs, Mam was busy at the kitchen table, wrapping a dish towel round a tray. There was another tray, already covered, beside her. I lifted a corner of the towel to find lots of Mowat's rolls, cut in two and filled with ham. I tucked the towel back where it had been and helped Mam carry the trays out to the pantry by the back door; she always said it was just as good as a fridge, being in the northeast corner of the house.

After breakfast, the three of us set off for the pier. Dad was in Lerwick, at the herring fishing, so couldn't be with us. The Street was busy with people heading for Blacksness, while, out on the water, sailing boats tacked their way through the voe.

We stopped at Williamson's to have a look at the trophies: cups and shields mainly, but my favourite was also there, a big silver boat with its sails up. When we moved on, it didn't take us long to reach the road by the castle from where we had our first sight of the crowd stretching along the edge of the pier below. Robina and I ran ahead.

The roadway took us past Hay's shops: the main one on the right where we ordered coal and bought the coarse salt Mam liked to lay whitings in for a day or so before she cooked them, and the little wooden shop on the left that was kept locked till you asked in the big shop. Robina and I had bought Mam an ornament there at Christmas; it was glass and in the shape of a house.

Further on were the fish processing sheds and, as we passed them, we heard a sound. Loud, but dull in tone, it told us that a boat had crossed the finishing line. At that, some spectators moved away, creating a gap that allowed us to find a spot right at the edge of the pier. I looked round to see if Mam had noticed where we were. She'd tell us to take care so close to the water, but for now she'd stopped and was talking to some people I didn't recognise. Visitors from all over Shetland came to the regatta.

In front of us, a line of boats stretched out over the water. We were able to see into the boats nearest the pier where crews of three made last-minute preparations for the next race, while, above their heads, sails flapped impatiently.

By the time Mam had caught up with us, the boats had moved off, a shifting line now as they competed to catch the wind on their way out the voe. Just then the *Hirta* appeared alongside the quay close to where we stood. She was Uncle Hancie's boat, offering trips to anyone who wished to have a closer look at how the boats got on, once they were out of sight of the shore.

"The swimming will be starting," Mam said, so we went with her, round the corner and past the harbour office where someone was playing *Indian Love Call* through loudspeakers attached to the outside wall.

"They always play that," I said. It was by Slim Whitman and I knew it well as it was one of the records we had for our wind-up gramophone with the picture of Little Miss Muffet on the lid, the one that had belonged to Robert. It was a present to him from Dad when he was peerie and Auntie Etta had wanted us to have it when Robert got a record player.

Just then, Mam spotted Auntie Jessie and Auntie Maggie among the crowd that was gathering at the edge of the pier – this was where the swimming took place, in water sheltered by two arms of the pier – so we joined our aunts. The women let Robina and me stand in front of them so we'd see better what was going on.

At some distance from us, a wooden pole jutted out over the water, a parcel done up in brown paper hanging from its outer end: the greasy pole. Nearby, the officials who'd start the races were already in position on a pontoon moored to the pier, and soon some swimmers appeared through the crowd to join them by way of a vertical iron ladder. It looked a long way down and must have been hard on bare feet too.

There were lots of races for the different age groups, with swimmers being cheered on by the onlookers.

Just as the last race was finishing, Mam said, "I'm going up to the house now. You stay and come up with Auntie Jessie and Auntie Maggie."

"But you'll miss the greasy pole," Robina said, however Mam had made up her mind. This event was the most entertaining bit as participants attempted to reach the brown paper parcel. The pole must have been very slippery as so many of them ended up in the water below. Eventually one man, who hadn't quite reached the parcel before beginning to slip, managed to grab it as he fell.

By the time we got up to the house, the kitchen table was covered in plates of bannocks and Mam was at the cooker heating up the soup. I could hear people talking and went in but to find Auntie Janie, Auntie Etta and Robert were already there. The settee and armchairs were pushed back from the fire and the chairs from the table under the window were arranged along the wall. The kitchen chairs had also been brought through and set out along with a couple of stools; Mam was still expecting lots of visitors.

Next to arrive was Rowena, then, through the window, I saw Uncle Walter and Auntie Mimie make their way up the path to the back door with Mimie's mother, Annie, and their visitors from sooth: Mimie's sister Ruby Ann, her husband Bill and their two children.

Once everyone was seated, Robina and I helped hand out bannocks while Mam ensured everyone had soup, some of it served in pudding plates when she ran out of soup plates. Empty plates were returned to the kitchen, where Auntie Jessie helped wash up so Mam could serve the newer arrivals: Auntie Annie Babsie with Elizabeth, James Andrew and Olive. They were followed by Auntie Tommy and her husband Walter, who had lingered on the pier to catch the end of a sailing race, and their family, Walter, Marjory and Ann. That made twenty-five of us in all, with teenagers and children required to sit on the floor.

Mam usually listened to the one o'clock news on the wireless, but there was no point today as conversation took over. This was one of the things I liked best about regatta day: the chat, the stories and the reminiscing, maybe even the odd difference of opinion. Among the things under discussion was whether or not Chris Chataway would take part in the sports in the afternoon. He'd been living in Scalloway for a while now and one day I'd even seen him in his shorts run down Meadowfield Road on the pavement opposite. When I told Dad I'd seen him, he'd said that Chataway was a famous runner and was probably practising to take part in the Olympics.

I helped take dishes back to the kitchen where Mam was filling the electric kettle. Once she'd switched it on, she picked up the old flat-bottomed kettle from its usual place on the back-to-back stove, topped it up with water and placed it on the cooker. She had two teapots standing ready too: the everyday one along with the heavily-patterned one that had been a wedding present and which came out only on special occasions. She fetched the ham rolls from the pantry so they could be passed round with cups of tea, though some of us had to wait till the electric kettle was boiled a second time.

There were plenty of volunteers to help with the washing up before people began to leave, some to return to the pier for the afternoon sailing and the rest to the park for the sports. That is where we were going, and Auntie Jessie and Auntie Maggie waited till we were ready, so instead of

The heavily-patterned one that had been a wedding present.

going in the top gate of the park, we went the long way round by the Street which made it easier for Auntie Maggie.

As we arrived, someone with a megaphone was calling runners to the next race. The park was busy, but Mam and her sisters were able to find a seat by the high wall on the New Road side, leaving Robina and me to wander off on our own.

First, we stopped at the peerie sand pit behind the swings, where the long jump was taking place. It was the turn of under-12 boys, so we knew several of them. Some had come prepared in shorts and sandshoes, but others competed in bare feet and trousers. One boy, who looked to have made a good jump, was upset to be disqualified for missing the mark where he should have jumped from.

"You've got two more tries," someone called out, but he still looked close to tears.

As we turned away from there, we noticed some children in pairs running along the edge of the park, arms round each other and with the left leg of one fastened to the right leg of the other at the ankles.

"We could do that," I said, "if Mam has something we could use to tie our legs together."Robina agreed and we ran back to find out.

"Mam, do you have a scarf?" I called out.

"What for?" she said.

"For the three-legged race," Robina replied as Mam pulled out a thin scarf from her pocket.

It was harder than it looked, even to move together without falling over, never mind pick up any speed, but we persevered and, when the three-legged race was called, we lined up with the others.

"Ready. Steady. Go," the starter called, and we moved off.

Right away, some children went into the lead. I concentrated hard on keeping in step with Robina and we managed about three-quarters of the distance before we tripped and fell. We weren't the only ones picking themselves up to get going again, even some of those who'd started quickly stumbled on their way to the finishing line. Mam had come over to watch the race so we were able to give her back her scarf before she returned to her seat.

The sack races and the egg-and-spoon races had finished, but there was still plenty going on. Robina and I watched the high jump for a while then found a spot on the edge of the park where we could see the running and keep a lookout for Chris Chataway, but I was looking forward most of all to the pillow fights. These were not for children and, as with the greasy pole at the pier, it seemed to be only men who took part. Two competitors sat on a long piece of wood, a bit like a telegraph pole, and hit each other with a large sack till one of them fell off.

This was an event that attracted a lot of spectators, so as soon as the pillow fights were announced, we ran over to get a place at the front of the crowd. With so many people gathered round, the cheering and laughter were loud and enthusiastic as one contestant after another was forced to retire. Eventually, there was only one man left and, to great applause, he was declared the winner. Still laughing at what we had seen, we picked ourselves up and went to watch the remaining races.

The last event was the mile race, eight times round the track, and this is the race some people said Chris Chataway would take part in. We got as near as we could to the start, but there was no sign of the star runner.

At the end of each race, there were money prizes for first, second and third place, but there was also a system of awarding points that counted towards championship prizes, one for men and one for women, but we didn't see those being presented right away. We'd have to wait till evening and the regatta concert for that.

Some of our relatives didn't want to attend the concert so returned to Burra on the *Tirrick*'s teatime run. When Robina and I got back to the house after the sports, Mam was already there, setting the table in but.

"Could you finish this?" she asked. "And I'll get back to the tea."

She'd spread the dark green chenille cloth then put a thinner one on top, but at an angle so the corners were green. I finished setting out the cutlery – the forks and ivory-handled knives she kept in the sideboard – then went into the kitchen.

Mam had bought plenty of eggs and sassermaet for ourselves and for those who hadn't gone back to Burra. As there were still too many of us to fit round one table, I helped set the kitchen table as well, using the cutlery that was kept in the kitchen.

As soon as the dishes were done, we left for the hall where there was already a queue at the door. The crowd was excited and chatty, with talk turning to Chris Chataway's non-appearance.

"They're saying he couldn't run because he can't accept cash prizes," someone said.

I wondered why he couldn't simply have run and turned down the money, but listening to the grown-ups, it seemed that hadn't been possible if he did wish to take part in the Olympics.

Eventually the doors opened and we got seats in the middle of the hall as it filled up. Below the stage, a table was set out with the trophies from Williamson's window. We'd soon find out which lucky skipper had won the silver ship. I looked round and saw that the partition at the back of the hall was open and the peerie hall set out with rows of chairs.

"Mam," I said, "where are our school desks?" Mam looked round.

"Maybe they've been taken upstairs for the summer," she said, "they always need the peerie hall for the regatta concert."

By the time the concert began, the hall was packed. The acts included sketches, singing, and a dance band. I was very pleased to see that Andy Irvine was taking part, he was so funny; Alan Anderson too, who did a funny song; and Alfie Harcus who played a tune on a saw.

When it was over, we said goodbye to some more of our visitors who left to catch a special run the *Tirrick* was doing.

Back in the house, Mam heated up some milk for Robina and me, then disappeared upstairs, returning with a pile of bedclothes. Meanwhile, our remaining visitors were getting ready for the dance that would soon be starting in the hall. Mam offered them cups of tea and sorted out the sleeping arrangements; there were too many for the beds upstairs so some were going to have to sleep on the but floor.

"You two," she then said, turning to Robina and me, "drink up; it's late."

As we headed for the but door, someone called out, "Goodnight."

"And it's been a good day," I replied.

CHAPTER SIXTEEN

The Pearls

It was too wet for us to go out to play. Robina sat at the table by the window, occasionally peering through the net curtains as if looking for a change in the weather, but mainly she seemed to be engrossed in her colouring book. I sat on the stool by the fire, my slippers kicked off and my feet on the hearthstone to keep warm.

I was holding my book in front of me, but keeping an eye on Mam, who sat in the chair opposite, counting loops in the jumper she was knitting. She'd got as far as the yoke and was preparing to set a Fair Isle pattern.

What particularly interested me were the two sacks on the floor beside her. They were made from a soft white cotton and bulged with cloos. When she'd finished counting, she removed the wire from her makkin belt and put down her work. She pulled one of the sacks closer and rolled down the top to reveal shades of fawn, brown, grey and white wool. Then she picked up the other bag and tipped its contents onto the floor. The round cloos spilled eagerly onto the mat: gold; mustard; lemon; peach; pale, soft and mid-blue; gentle greens; a touch of red – not scarlet to scream at the others, but more subdued. There were duller colours too: deep red, indigo, navy and dark green.

Leaving my book on the stool, I got down on my knees to help her select the ten or twelve colours she'd need for the yoke. The more sombre hues lit up as they were paired with the brighter ones, a colour for the background and a colour for the pattern. I picked up her chosen colours and unrolled a length of yarn from each cloo before wrapping it round its partner to keep them together. She lined up the pairs in the order she'd

My pearl ring.

use them, trying various combinations until she was satisfied with the overall appearance.

Once she'd made her final selection, we replaced the unwanted cloos in the bags and prepared to return them to the linen cupboard upstairs.

"Are you coming?" I asked Robina.

She nodded, put down her crayons and slipped off the seat. Mam went first, carrying one of the bags, then Robina and then me with the other bag. We had to go in that order as Robina was too small to be allowed in the stairs on her own.

The linen cupboard was close to the top of the stairs. Mam opened the door and stepped inside. The cupboard always smelled fresh, a combination of distemper on the walls and the clean towels, tablecloths and bedclothes on the slatted shelves running up two sides. You couldn't see what some of the stuff was as Mam had covered it up using old curtains. I imagined those mysterious bundles were maybe her 'best' towels and bedclothes for the spare room.

The only bit that we were allowed access to was under the shelves, where cardboard boxes containing our toys and games were kept, but today I had something else in mind. As Mam stowed the white bags on the second shelf, I slipped through to the spare room and went over to the fireplace. I stepped onto the hearth and carefully removed a small trinket box from the narrow mantelpiece. The box was made of some kind of glazed white pottery, with a hinged lid that fastened with a little metal clasp. On the top it said *A Present from Lerwick* alongside a picture of a woman in a very tall black hat, although I'd never seen such a hat in Lerwick. I looked inside to check the contents; all the usual things were there – a kirby grip, a badge, some kind of brooch in the shape of an aeroplane and a couple of small greyish lumps that Mam said were pearls.

Being careful not to drop it, I carried the box back to where Mam was waiting while Robina rummaged among our toys in the foot of the linen cupboard.

"Tell us about the pearls, Mam," I begged, handing her the box.

"Can I look?" Robina turned round to ask.

Mam held the box so she could see inside it. "Let's go downstairs first," she said.

"When I was young," she began, "the men didn't use nets to catch haddock."

"They used lines," I interrupted. Dad had been at the line fishing, the year before.

"That's right," she said, "but it's very unusual nowadays and, another thing, you'll remember that Dad baited his own lines, but it used to be the women and girls who did all that."

"Girls?" I said. "What age were you?"

"About sixteen," she replied.

"On their way ashore, the men dredged yoag shells up from the bottom and it was our job to open them, so we could cut up the flesh for bait," she explained.

"And the shells?" I broke in. I knew what happened to the shells. We'd heard the story so often it was as familiar as the stories in my books, but I wanted Mam to tell us again.

"The shells were crushed onto paths, so it didn't get too muddy underfoot."

"Like the Shelly Road in Hamnavoe," I exclaimed.

"In Hamnavoe," Robina said. Mam often called her a parrot.

"That's right," Mam smiled. She seemed to like the story too.

"We had a large knife to work with, but sometimes it was difficult to open the shells. The worst bit of all was dealing with the lines. They were in a fearsome tangle when they came ashore and we had to redd them first, being very careful not to get the hooks caught in our fingers."

"Was it sore?" Robina asked.

"It would hurt you, coming back out," Mam explained, "because of the way the barbs faced in opposite directions."

I shuddered; I'd seen fishhooks.

"Were they Faider's lines?" That was what we'd called Mam's dad.

"No, it was Robbie o' Clate's lines."

"Did he let you keep the pearls?" I wondered.

She laughed, "Nobody wanted them."

I never understood that bit. "Did you find lots of pearls?" I continued. "What about the other girls; did they find any?"

"Most people threw them away," Mam always said that as well; it was the most puzzling bit of all.

"Some of them were too small or too black," she went on, "but I kept these," she added, holding out the trinket box, "and when you're big girls, I'm going to take the pearls and my gold watch that has broken, the one your father gave me when we were young, to Mr Rae, so he can make rings from the watch strap and set the pearls in them. And when you wear the rings, these dull pearls will become polished and start to shine."

Robina was playing with her dolls' tea set and I was back on the stool, reading. Mam stood up; it was time to make the tea. As she moved away from her chair, a pair of cloos tumbled to the floor. A dark fawn brightened by a pretty peach; the same kind of magic that would happen to the grey pearls.

CHAPTER SEVENTEEN

What's in a Name?

I t was a coorse winter's day, wet and so windy that Dad had been ashore all day. He had been down at the pier, but was back now and sitting reading by the fire. School was over for the day so Robina and I were at home, forced by the weather to remain indoors. At the table under the front window, first we played Snakes and Ladders then we played Snap till Robina said she wanted to do something else and got out her colouring book.

I gathered the cards together and laid out a game of Patience, but my mind wasn't on it; there was something I wanted to ask. "Dad," I said, "what age was I when we left Burra?"

With my parents in Hamnavoe.

I didn't remember the move. From repeated visits to Burra, I knew the house we'd stayed in well; it was the house Dad had been brought up in, and Mam had moved there after they married.

"You were nearly two;" Dad replied, "your second birthday was just a month after we came here."

"Why?" I asked. "Why did we move?"

"Because the house was too small," he said. "There was you, your Mam and me, Etta and Robert, and Granda."

I moved from the table to sit on the stool beside his chair. "And Grandmam," I said.

Grandmam had been Granda's wife and Dad's mother, but I didn't remember her and wasn't sure whether or not she'd been alive when we moved. I knew what she looked like from a photo of her and Granda on the wall of the spare bedroom. They stood together, dressed in dark clothes, in front of a door that was coloured green. Granda was leaning away from my grandmother, his right hand reaching down to pat a brown collie that was looking up at them both.

Dad said the dog was named Carlo, but it was Grandmam's name I was interested in. She'd been known as Willa Katie and Mam had told me that was the same as my name, Williamina Catherine. Even though I didn't care for my full name, I was curious to know more about my grandmother.

Dad paused. Was he going to tell me anything, I wondered.

"She died," he said.

I knew that, but asked, "When?"

After another pause, Dad continued, "Just before you were born."

"What?" I said. "The same day?"

"No," he replied, "on 17th."

That was just four days before my birthday, but Dad hadn't finished, "That's why you were born at Duke Street," he went on.

Duke Street was where Mam had been brought up and she had told me previously that I'd been born in her old home, but it had never struck me till now just how odd that was. The more usual thing would've been for me to be born at Granda's where Mam and Dad were living.

"We thought you'd be born on the 20th," he went on, "but that was Grandmam's funeral day, so we thought it would be better if Mam went home to her mam to wait for you to turn up."

"What happened?" I asked.

"You didn't appear on the 20th," Dad said, and explained that I'd been born at about half past three the next morning, then added, "and that means

Grandmam and Granda.

you've been running three and a half hours late ever since." He smiled, he was teasing me, the same way Auntie Etta did.

"Why did she die?" I asked.

"She was in hospital;" he said, "she'd had an operation and got something called a clot."

I didn't understand.

"It might have been better if she'd been allowed to move about, but that was forbidden at the time," he said.

"That's sad," I said. Dad looked thoughtful. Just then Mam came through from the kitchen, the door had been open and she'd heard some of what we'd been saying.

"And when your Dad saw you," Mam said, "he said, 'We don't have to think what to call this one.'" I smiled and for the first time felt more accepting of my full name. I still didn't like it, but I understood it better.

There didn't seem to be anything more to say so I returned to my game of Patience.

"It'll soon be teatime," Mam said, and disappeared back into the kitchen.

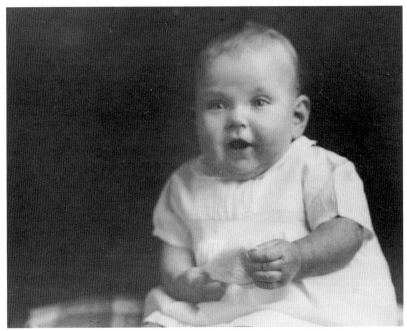

Me. *Photo by C J Williamson, courtesy of Willie Smith*

CHAPTER EIGHTEEN

Food for Thought

The boats were at sea again, but it was another disappointing day of weather on land, so after school, instead of playing outside, Robina and I had once again been driven indoors by a heavy shower. Mam was now busy in the kitchen, Robina fully occupied with her dolls' house, and I was at a loose end. I'd finished my library book, but wouldn't get a replacement till it was once more the turn of my class to make a selection from the bookcase in the school corridor.

I looked round the room and my eye was caught by the ship in a bottle that sat on the shelf behind Dad's chair. The bottle was square-shaped and lay on its side, as best suited the model it contained – a black-hulled ship battling through heavy seas in an icy landscape. It had lain there for as long as I could remember and I knew a little of its story: the boat was a Hull trawler – the *White Thorn* – that Dad had been on during the Second World War after she was requisitioned by the Navy and sent to Iceland.

Time to have a closer look, so I squeezed between Dad's chair and the wireless. I knew I wasn't allowed to lift the bottle down from the shelf, so stood where I was, once more taking in the details of the ship and its little white flag that had what looked like a Union Jack in one corner, the angry waves and the snow-covered land with a house and a lighthouse down by the shore.

That shore gave me an idea, so I opened the kitchen door and asked, "Mam, can I look at the old photo album?"

She turned from the sink, a quizzical look on her face.

"To see that photo you sent Dad when he was away," I explained, "and the Iceland post cards."

Mam smiled. "You know where it is," she said.

I returned to the living room, opened the door at one end of the sideboard and removed a small photo album before reaching for the old bulky one that held what I was looking for.

We'd often had a look through the album, so I knew that the Iceland post cards were at the back and turned there first. There were four in all: one showed a waterfall; another, a place named Siglufjörður; and the remaining two were of a town called Akureyri.

I now had another question for Mam, so back in the kitchen I asked, "Were there Germans in Iceland?"

"Don't think so," Mam replied.

"What was Dad doing there then?"

"You'll have to ask him," was Mam's reply.

She was still busy preparing the tea, but I hadn't finished. "Was he there for the whole war?"

"For thirteen months," Mam said, "right after he was called up in 1941; just after we got married."

Thirteen months seemed like a long time; no wonder she'd sent a photo to him.

I went back to the album and flicked through the pages till I found it: a studio photo, taken by Clement Williamson. It showed Mam half-sitting, half-leaning against what looked like the same box-shaped piece of furniture that Robina and I had sat on to have our photos taken when Robina was just a year old. In this photo, Mam was wearing a dress that came below her knee; it was dark-coloured with some decoration on the

A black-hulled ship battling through heavy seas in an icy landscape.

Dad in 1946, when he was demobbed.

The photo Mam sent to Dad in 1941. *Photo by C J Williamson, courtesy of Willie Smith*

yoke and at the waist though I couldn't decide whether or not it also had a belt. There was a fancy background with ornate windows, but I knew those weren't real.

I had another question.

This time I interrupted Mam getting cutlery out of the drawer in the kitchen table. "When was that photo taken? The one you sent Dad."

"Just after Dad went away," she replied. "Now give me a hand to set the table. I had the photo taken specially to send him."

Dad managed to be home by teatime, so I asked him about Iceland and he told us all about the marksmen on board the *White Thorn* who shot at the enemy mines to make holes in them so they'd fill with water and sink.

"I only once saw one of those mines explode," he said. "I was home on leave and happened to be out at the front of the house when one was swept onto the rocks behind the lighthouse."

He then told us about the young naval officer on the *White Thorn* whose task it was to assemble some equipment each morning and how Dad was detailed to help.

"Even with a book of instructions, he struggled," Dad said, "so I said to him to put his book away and let me do it."

Mam with Dad in 1946, when he was demobbed.

"But why were you there at all? Mam said there were no ..." I began.

"The Germans had laid the mines to deter the Russian convoys," Dad explained, "boats going the long way round from the west coast of Scotland to Russia."

"Why were you just called up in 1941?" I asked.

"Because of my age," he said. "When the war began, lots of younger people were called up, but I was allowed to stay at home."

"What age were you," I asked, "when the war started?"

"I was born in 1908," he said.

That was easy. "Thirty-one," I said.

"That's right," he replied, "when the war began, but later on they needed men for the convoys."

At this point, Mam took up the story. "It just happened that the convoys began at the same time we got married, so it was only two weeks after the wedding that Dad got his calling up papers."

She then went on to tell us how, after Dad came back from Iceland, he was posted to various places on the east side of the country and how she'd stayed with him in billets in Arbroath and in South Queensferry. There were also post cards of those places in the album.

"Were you away till the war ended?" I asked her.

"I didn't go to England with him," she said. "I was home before D-Day."

Dad then went on to tell us that he'd been on a small tanker, the *Libya*, that crossed the English Channel on the 6th June, 1944, and how, when he went to the deck rail to collect supplies of food from a vessel that was delivering provisions to the fleet, a crew member on the other boat had said, "We don't have enough for everyone. Half of you are supposed to be dead."

Before bedtime, I had another look at the photo album, this time looking for pictures of Dad in naval uniform. When I found them, I couldn't help but look over at the glass bottle and the black ship and the turbulent seas before considering the man who hadn't had enough food for everyone.

The day might not have gone as Robina and I had hoped, but Mam and Dad had certainly given us much to think about.

CHAPTER NINETEEN

Taking Part

Mam was at the kitchen sink when I found her.

"Do we have any more crêpe paper?" I asked. It was Saturday and there was a job I wanted getting on with.

"In the cupboard," she said, with a nod towards but.

I knew she meant the cupboard just inside the but door. It was tall, almost reaching the ceiling, with glass doors in the top half where there were lots of books, though in its lowermost shelf Mam kept teasets and ornaments. Below that was a pair of wooden doors with small smooth knobs, almost green in colour, and one of those doors was, I knew, already standing open. Among the things kept there – Mam's makkin, her makkin belt, the jotter with her patterns dotted down, even the iron – were the remnants of some rolls of crêpe paper.

"It's the wrong colour," I said.

She turned round. She had a nylon pot scrubber in her hands. She was cleaning the sink with Ajax, the way she did every day after denner. "What do you need?" she asked. "What's it for?"

"The gala," I said, "for my bike. I'll need pink, but there's just red and yellow."

It was Scalloway Football Club's gala the next weekend and I'd decided to decorate my bike so I could take part in the procession.

"Is that all there is?" she asked.

"There's white," I replied, "that'll do, but I need colours, and red and yellow will clash."

My bike was cerise, Mam said, and that didn't go with red – or with yellow. "Can I go and buy some?" I asked.

Soon I was on my way to Melody Corner, situated next to the milk shop on the Street. The sign above the door was in the shape of a guitar with lettering on it that read: *Tobacco, Sweets, Books and Stationery*. I went in and asked for crêpe paper. They had lots of colours and I was pleased to see a dark pink like my bike and a baby pink, so took a roll of each.

Back home, I asked Mam for the Sellotape and a loan of the scissors before sitting down at the kitchen table to open up the rolls of paper. Roll didn't seem to be the right word for something so flat, but its shape did make it easy to handle. I undid a length of the dark pink, but allowed it to fold itself up according to the creases that were already there. When I judged there was enough for my needs, I reached for the scissors. They felt odd in my hand, the paper reluctant to yield to the metal and it needed a

Me and my bike. *Photo by W Williamson, courtesy of Elizabeth Marshall*

lot of concentration to keep a straight line along the full length of the roll. I repeated this with the other two rolls till I had produced what amounted to a thin roll of each colour. The next step was to cut each of these into slices a few inches deep.

This meant cutting through several thicknesses at once, but giving the scissors more to do, somehow made them easier to control and I soon had several pieces of each pink, along with some white, ready to transform my bike. I helped myself to the shed key from its hook on the side of the kitchen dresser, picked up the pieces of crêpe paper, the Sellotape and the scissors, and headed for the door.

"I'm going out to the shed," I said to Mam, who was replacing something in the broom cupboard, "will I need the power on?"

Mam looked out the window. "Maybe," she said, then added, "I'll put it on for you."

Davie had fixed lights and sockets in the shed, but the cleverest thing was the handy switch in the cupboard by the front door where the meter was, and that was for switching power on and off to the shed only. It was also a good way of signalling to Dad that it was time to come in when the tea was ready.

But Dad was at Nicolson's shop, paying for the papers and buying cigarettes for himself, Quality Street for Mam and Cadbury's Dairy Milk chocolate for Robina and me – at least that is what I hoped; that is what he usually did on a Saturday. Anyway, I was able to use his bench to work on and to prop my bike up against.

I didn't think I needed the lights on yet, so got on with cutting off some Sellotape to fasten a piece of the dark pink crêpe paper to the top of the frame, below the handlebars. Kneeling down, I began winding the paper around the frame as it sloped diagonally downwards, leaving spaces where the frame showed through in between each circling. I was lucky and reached the bottom before running out of paper, but just as I reached for the Sellotape again, the whole thing unravelled from the top. The Sellotape had come off the crêpe paper.

I wasn't entirely surprised. I knew how difficult it had been to stick Sellotape to crêpe paper when making Christmas decorations at school, but this was serious. I had to find a way of getting the crêpe paper to remain in place for the procession.

"Mam," I called out, as I went in the back door. She wasn't in the kitchen, but I found her in but. She'd decided the big cupboard needed tidying.

"Do you have something I could use to keep the crêpe paper on the bike; it's just fallen off?"

Mam shook her head. "What kind of something?" she asked. "You can't put glue on your bike. Can you tie it on?"

"I don't want string," I said. "That would spoil it."

"Thread," Mam suggested.

"Do you have pink?" I asked.

"In my workbox," she said.

This was a basket that stood in a corner of the kitchen dresser, so I fetched it and had a good look among the pirms of thread. There was no pink, just a dark red. I looked at the label: 'Burgundy'.

"Isn't this too dark?" I asked.

"No," Mam said, "better to be darker; like sewing on a button."

I wasn't sure what she meant; sewing was not my favourite pastime.

Back in the shed, I wrapped a length of crêpe paper round the frame as before, but instead of Sellotape, this time I used thread that I tied tightly round the top and bottom of the paper. Hoping that it would hold, I moved on to another part of the frame where I did exactly the same and stood back.

The first piece of crêpe paper was slipping out from under the thread.

"Mam," I was back in the house, "that was no use. The thread isn't holding it."

"So what are you going to do now?" she asked.

"Could I fix the thread to the paper somehow?" I was thinking aloud. "Could I sew it?" I asked. "Put a few stitches in the paper, I mean, and leave long ends for tying. Can I try that?"

Mam shook her head again, but she was smiling. "If you think it'll work," she agreed.

The workbox was still in but, so I picked out a needle and rummaged for another pirm, a white one this time, then fetched the remains of the white crêpe paper roll from where I'd left it in on the kitchen table. It wouldn't matter if I made holes in a small bit of it. The needle went through the paper quite easily and I took a few stitches before pulling the thread out again. This was more fun than school sewing.

When I left the house a third time, I was aware that the sky had darkened; time to put the lights on in the shed. Back at the bench, I used burgundy thread to stitch across the end of a strip of the dark pink, leaving a few inches of thread free at each side. I then used the thread to tie the paper as tightly as possible to the top of the frame before winding the rest of the strip on as before.

This approach was promising, but I noticed that the holes made by the needle were stretching, so perhaps I shouldn't stitch quite so close to the end of the paper. But more worryingly, the paper had also slid down a fraction. I needed an anchor point where the thread could be tied in such a way that the paper wouldn't slip.

I removed the paper strip once more and threaded the needle with a longer piece of thread. After I'd stitched the paper, a good inch away from the end this time, I tied the thread round the bare metal strut below the handlebars where a large nut would keep it in place. Finally, I'd found a way to proceed that would survive for the time the procession took to get from Blacksness to the west shore then wind its way back to the park.

I was still busy with needle and paper when the lights went off for a second or two before coming on again. Teatime already.

Dad was home, so, while we were having our tea, I told him what I was up to. "I used two different colours round the frame," I said. "I left space the first time then filled that in with the second colour. Like a barber's pole, though I've not used all that much white; it's mostly been pink and a dark pink, like the bike. You can come and see it after teatime."

Then I turned to Mam. "Do you have anything else I can use on the bike?"

"What do you mean?" she asked.

"Something fancy," I said.

"We'll see after tea," she replied.

It was Robina's and my job to do the tea dishes and tonight it was my turn to dry and put things away. Just my luck, when I was so keen to get back to the bike.

Mam came through from but. "Will this do?" she said. She was holding some paper doilies in her hand. She didn't use them very often and I'd never seen these particular ones; they were shiny.

"They're silver," I said.

"Yes," said Mam. "Not sure where they came from. Can you make use of them?"

"Can I cut them up?" I asked.

Back in the shed, I considered what I'd done so far. The main sections of the frame were finished and I'd begun wrapping the crêpe paper round the narrow struts that ran down to the centre of the back wheel. Those looked better with thinner strips of crêpe paper and I'd spent a lot of time getting the width right. I knew I should finish that off, but it was fiddly and I was keen to work out how to use the doilies, so picked up the scissors.

With scissors in one hand and a doily in the other, it was difficult to know how to continue; the circular shape and scalloped edges called for a new approach. I looked again at the bike, more critically this time. The crêpe paper was concentrated on the centre of the bike so the mudguards, particularly the back one, stood out in their undecorated state. I began to cut.

From the centre of the doily, I removed a section that was as long as the doily was wide, yet narrow enough to fit onto the mudguard. Using Sellotape, I was able to fix this silver strip to the rear mudguard starting just above the red reflector then, once again, stood back to see the effect.

I was pleased with the way the dark pink colour of the bike showed through the holes, so reached for another doily to attach a similarly sized piece to the front mudguard. The shorter pieces of doily that were left over, I cut to produce small patches of silver along the remaining lengths of both mudguards.

That bit completed, I was busy with the crêpe paper once more when the shed door opened. It was Dad, come to see how I was getting on.

"I've almost finished here," I said, "though I am running out of crêpe paper."

"Will you be able to ride the bike with all that on it?" Dad asked.

"I'll be pushing it," I replied. "The procession doesn't go that quickly and I might have to have a collecting tin too."

Spectators threw money onto the floats, but I'd also seen people on foot with tins.

Dad came back to the house when I went in for more crêpe paper and soon after that, my bike was ready for the gala.

It was a nice warm evening when I set off for Blacksness, pushing my bike with care so as not to dislodge or damage any of the decoration. It was a long way to the Street and the east shore, then on past Clement's and Wilfie's, but eventually I reached the roadway outside the castle. From here, I could see there was already a lot of activity ahead as people milled about on the pier, many in fancy dress.

I continued down the brae and, once past the fish factory and other buildings, was able to see the floats waiting in line, some with musicians already on board. After a quick look at the various vehicles, I moved over to join the throng that was concentrated close to the edge of the pier.

The start of Scalloway Gala. Robina and me on right hand side, Mam behind us, in headscarf.
Photo by C J Williamson, courtesy of Willie Smith

Requiring a spot where no harm would come to my bike meant that I ended up on the fringes of the crowd, but I still got a glimpse of a dark hull approaching before someone shouted, "Here she is!"

This was followed by another cry of, "Look out!" as an open-top car appeared, making its way slowly through the crowd to park parallel to the edge of the pier.

Once it had stopped, everyone pushed forward again. The boat came alongside and a path was cleared so the passengers could make their way to the car; the Gala Queen and her attendants had arrived, as usual, by sea from the Point.

The crowd thinned as participants took their places on the floats. I wheeled my bike over to the start and joined a group that would be following on foot. Some of them had collecting tins, but I didn't see any spare ones so I'd have to do without.

Amid music, noise and bustle, the procession set off up the pier. Along New Street, people came out of their houses to cheer us on and another crowd was waiting when we reached the Street. Although I didn't have the means to collect money myself, I was kept busy retrieving pennies from the ground where they'd fallen short of the floats, then throwing them onto the nearest lorry myself.

At the west shore, we turned into the steep slopes of Hillside Road. There weren't so many people lining the route here, which was just as well as I had to concentrate hard on guiding my bike while avoiding the wheels of the lorries. From the whines of their engines, which threatened to drown out the musicians, the lorries, too, appeared to be struggling.

There was a tight turn at the top into Houl Road, but after that the engines' notes became calmer; it was downhill now, all the way to the Co-op corner where we rejoined the Street. At the park gates, the Gala Queen's car turned in so the Queen could meet both teams before the football began.

The floats continued along the Street; they'd be heading for Blacksness where they'd be dismantled, but I decided there was no point in my following and wheeled my bike into the park.

Just before teatime a few days later, Robina and I were sitting at the table in but playing a game of Snakes and Ladders when we heard the click of the front gate.

"It's John Macdonald," I called through to Mam who was in the kitchen, "is there any money in the box?"

John Macdonald was our Sunday School superintendent, but he also was responsible for collecting any money that had been put into the Methodist Home Missions box that stood on the same shelf as the ship in the bottle.

Before Mam could answer, John Macdonald had come in the back door and I heard them speaking before they came through.

"It's you he wants to see," Mam said, looking at me.

"That's right," John Mac said, holding out an envelope. "You won second prize for decorating your bike."

I didn't know what to say, but he went on, "It looked lovely, but the judges thought it would be better giving first prize to a bike decorated in Scalloway colours."

After he'd gone, I asked Mam why it was John Macdonald who'd come with my prize.

"He's secretary of the football club," she said. Then added, "You didn't look very pleased with your prize. Do you think you should've won?"

"Won!" I said. "I didn't even know I was in a competition."

CHAPTER TWENTY

Moving On

"It's Saturday," I said to myself, prompted by the smell of baking that was drifting upstairs. A school morning meant gruel, but Saturday was when Mam baked and, if I hurried, I'd have a nice warm bannock with a cup of milk for breakfast.

Soon, I was pushing open the door into the kitchen where I found Mam busy at the table, a large baking bowl in front of her and, at the end of the table, a pile of newly-baked bannocks, half-hidden in a tea towel. As I watched, Mam separated a piece of dough from the mixture in the bowl and placed it on a rectangular sheet of oilcloth cut from the same fabric as the cloth that covered the table.

The cloth was already floured and Mam now scattered some more flour on the dough as well before working it into a shape like a partially collapsed football. Next, she picked up the empty glass bottle she kept as a rolling pin and rolled the dough out into a flat circle. The last stage before baking was to cut this circle in two before picking up one half and taking it over to the cooker.

Warning me not to come too close, she placed the bannock on a wire rack that straddled the large rectangular hotplate, already heated up for the purpose. Some of the loose flour fell through the wire and onto the hotplate where it sparked red for a second then vanished, black ash on a black plate. The rack may have been designed for cooling, but put to this use, it was hot, very hot, and Mam had to be careful as she placed the second bannock beside the first.

Once she judged the underside to be done, Mam had a way of turning the bannock with the aid of a knife without burning herself. At this point, I moved away from the cooker to get out a plate and a knife as well as a cup into which I poured myself some milk before sitting down at the table.

There was butter and treacle on the table, either of which I could have spread on one of the bannocks already baked, but I wanted one that was freshly off the cooker – and I didn't have long to wait. Soon, Mam deftly picked up a bannock from the cooker and transferred it to my plate. Instead of splitting the bannock, I placed a small amount of butter on its floury surface and watched as the solid mass of yellow melted and ran along the indentations left by the wire.

"You don't use a recipe," I said. "How do you know what to do?"

Mam laughed. "I've always made bannocks," she replied.

"Did Midder teach you?" Midder was how we referred to Mam's mother who died when I was only four years old and it so happened that my only memory of her was seeing her bake bannocks on an American stove.

"She showed me how," Mam said.

"And Auntie Jessie," I went on.

"Yes, all the lasses." Mam meant all four of her sisters.

"And Auntie Etta and her sisters," I asked, "would Grandmam have shown them how to bake?"

"I expect so," Mam replied.

Thinking about those family members, prompted me to ask, "Tell me again about our move from Burra."

By now, all the dough was used up and Mam was mixing a brönnie. This was a richer mix with egg and fruit in it which would be put in a tin and baked in the oven. However, working with it didn't prevent her from continuing the conversation.

"Granda wanted us to build an extension on the house so we could stay, but your Dad thought that might spoil the look of the house and, besides, he was saving hard to buy a share in another boat."

"What do you mean, another boat?" I asked.

"He had a share in a boat before the war, but it was requisitioned."

"Like the *White Thorn*," I said.

"Smaller," Mam said, "but the same idea, and when the war ended they didn't get much money. Reparation, they called it, but it wasn't enough for a share."

"Dad said that, after I was born, the house was too small," I said.

"That's right, no-one expected that your Auntie Etta would have to return to the family home."

Photo by C J Williamson, courtesy of Willie Smith

Scalloway, with the Crudens under construction.

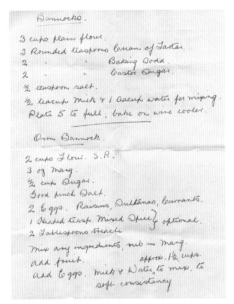

Mam's recipes for bannocks and brönnies (oven bannocks). Me, aged two after we moved to Scalloway. *Photo by C J Williamson, courtesy of Willie Smith*

I knew this bit of the story: when Dad's four sisters got married they moved out, but Auntie Etta hadn't been married long when her husband lost his life and she'd gone back to live with Granda and Grandmam.

"So it was all to do with the war, our move," I said.

"I suppose so," said Mam, "but we weren't the only ones looking for new homes at that time ..."

"... and the council built them here," I finished her sentence. I knew that, on our side of the road, up as far as the junction with Craigpark Road, the houses were all occupied by folk from Burra – or Trondra, in the case of Vivian's Dad.

"That's right," said Mam, "they wouldn't put them in Burra as there was neither running water nor electricity at the time."

"But they've got those things now," I said.

"Yes," said Mam, "they started the water scheme just a year after we left, then the power was switched on a year or two after that."

I liked our house with its red slate roof and funny little open porch at the front door. The porch roof was also red, as were the bricks arranged at angles along the paths: a splash of colour along one side of Meadowfield Road.

"And Dad said they're not just here, the Crudens."

While we'd been speaking, Mam had lined the oven tin with grease-proof paper and scraped the brönnie mixture into it.

As she replied to me, she moved away from the table to open the oven door. "That's right," she said, "lots of these houses were built all over Scotland after the war."

The mixing bowl and wooden spoon were still on the table; I pulled them towards me. "Can I lick the spoon?" I asked. I'd finished my breakfast.

Mam nodded and said, "When you're done with it, put it in the sink, then go and waken your sister."

Burra Scalloway bairns, back from left: The author and Ivor Jamieson. Front from left: Rena Fraser, Linda Williamson and Robina.

CHAPTER TWENTY-ONE

A Short Visit

"Remember, get home as quickly as you can," Mam said, as we left to make our way back to school for the afternoon.

Robina and I assured her we hadn't forgotten that we were going to Burra for the weekend. At least Mam, Robina and I were; Dad was at the herring fishing so we wouldn't see him till tomorrow, Saturday.

When lessons came to an end, I fetched my coat from the cloakroom and hurried out the door. Robina's class got out before mine, so she'd already be home. When I got back, Mam was in the kitchen where she'd set the table for tea, but there was to be no sitting down yet.

"Did you look out some things to take with you?" Mam asked.

"Yes," I replied, "my book and a colouring book and pencils – and some *Girls* for Marjory and Ann."

The *Girl* was my comic and I loved reading the stories it contained: 'Belle of the Ballet', 'Jinx and Wendy', and 'Lettice Leefe', but my favourite was 'Vicky', who travelled to all sorts of interesting places and had great adventures.

"Go and put them in the case; it's in but," Mam said, then added, "I've already packed your Sunday clothes along with your words."

She meant the slips of paper our Sunday School teachers had given us for the Sunday School Anniversary. We'd had a special anniversary service in Scalloway this past Sunday, but each year it was repeated in Burra and that's why we were going now, even though it wasn't a school holiday.

When I'd done that, I returned to the kitchen. Mam was slicing bread. "You'll have to get changed;" she said, "I've laid out some clothes that'll do tomorrow as well."

"Can I go to the pictures tomorrow night?" I asked.

"Catherine, we need our time," was all the reply I got. I'd have to ask again, later.

Once I'd changed and was back downstairs, the tea was ready: boiled eggs, not my favourite, but with the help of buttered strips of bread I ate the yolk and managed an egg-spoonful or two of white. Once we'd finished eating, and Mam had washed up, she told us to go and get our coats as Hindie's car would soon be here. The case had Dad's Sunday suit in it as well as all our things and that made it too heavy for Mam to carry all the way to Blacksness.

At the pier, the boats for Burra were waiting: the *Madge* that connected Scalloway to Bridge End, the white launch for Papil, and the *Tirrick* which we'd be taking to Hamnavoe. Uncle Hancie was on the *Tirrick*'s deck and, when he saw us, he fetched the brown box from the wheelhouse, the one that was both seat and set of steps. With it in place, he reached for

Ready for Sunday School with our second cousin Elizabeth, right.

Photo by W Williamson, courtesy of Elizabeth Marshall

the suitcase from Mam then helped us on board. Mam always liked to sit in the wheelhouse so that's where we went, taking a seat on the padded cushions.

Soon, through the wheelhouse door, we caught sight of Johnson's teatime bus approaching down the pier. After it came to a stop, lots of Burra folk got off and headed for one or other of the ferries. Among the crowd, I spotted my cousin Walter; he was at the Lerwick school and I knew this was him heading home for the weekend. I saw him come on board, but didn't see where he went after that, so either he stayed on deck or went down to the cabin. When some grown-ups came into the wheelhouse, Mam made us stand so they could have a seat.

The engine was already running so, once everyone was on board and the brown box back in the wheelhouse, the *Tirrick* cast off and we were on our way, with Uncle Hancie at the wheel and Andrew perched on the makeshift seat beside him.

The weather was fine and the crossing, smooth; this suited Mam who wasn't a good sailor. After a bit, Uncle Hancie handed over the wheel to Andrew and began to collect fares. Mam opened her purse, ready to pay, but as usual, Uncle Hancie ignored her and collected from the others before leaving the wheelhouse to take up the rest of the fares.

When we got to Hamnavoe, we went straight to Granda's where Auntie Etta had a cup of hot water ready for Mam to drink. Mam always had this after being on a boat; she said it helped her stomach. I'd tried drinking the hot water once to see what it was like, but it didn't appeal to me; it seemed to have a different taste from cold water and not one that I liked.

After a bit, Mam must have been feeling better because she picked up the case and said she was going to unpack it. I followed her to retrieve my book and other belongings.

"Take your sister's things too," Mam said.

I noticed that Robina had also brought a colouring book. Just then Auntie Etta came through to show Mam where she could hang up our Sunday things.

I found Robina in but with Granda who was reading the paper. While Robina got on with colouring in, I found where I was up to in my book. It was by Enid Blyton; I'd read all the 'Secret Seven' stories I could get my hands on and was now reading about the 'Famous Five'. One of the five was a dog belonging to the main character, a girl who had her hair cut very short and called herself George. The others were George's cousins and together they got into all kinds of scrapes involving crooks and spies and treasure. I hadn't got far yet with this one in which George had run away from home after her father laughed at the dog.

I was still reading when Auntie Etta brought drinks of warm milk for Robina and me. Mam said it was time to go to bed, but I was reluctant to give up on my book where George had been joined by her cousin Anne and the two were camping in an isolated spot. They'd met a mysterious boy and his little dog, and seen strange lights coming from a ruined cottage. I had to know what happened next.

"You can read some more tomorrow," Mam said.

This reminded me. "I'd like to go to the pictures tomorrow night," I said.

"Do you know what's on?" Mam asked.

"No," I said, looking at Auntie Etta, but she didn't seem to know either – I loved going to the pictures just as much as I liked reading and knew that, when there were Highlands and Islands' films in Scalloway on a Thursday, the same films were shown in Hamnavoe on the Saturday, but this wasn't their week. The Burra Hall Committee would have booked their own films this time, "But I'll find out."

The next day, I asked Mam, "Can I take the comics up to Auntie Tommy's?"

It wasn't far and Robina came with me. We found our aunt in the back getting their denner ready, but she stopped to have a word with us. "I heard you were coming," she said, and asked us about Mam and Dad.

"Dad'll be coming on the denner time boat," I replied, then asked if Marjory and Ann were in.

"They're in but," she said, so we went through. The girls were playing cards, but when they saw I'd brought copies of the *Girl*, they stopped and looked out a pile of their comics, *The Girls' Crystal* and *The School Friend*, in exchange.

"Are you going to the pictures?" I asked.

"Yes," said Marjory. "It's a cowboy film. Are you going?"

"I hope so;" I said, "I'll have to ask."

Just then Auntie Tommy called the girls through for their denner and we left.

"It's cowboys and Indians;" I said to Mam as soon as we got back to Granda's, "Marjory and Ann are going."

"All right," said Mam, "now go and play till it's time to eat."

"Can we go and meet the boat, first?" I asked. Mam agreed to that too so I sat down with the comics until it was time to head for the pier.

Robina and I waited at the top of the pier where, as usual, a lot of people and several vehicles had gathered. When the *Tirrick* came into view, we found it hard to make out Dad among the dark-clad crowd of men on the deck: herring fishermen, returning from the east side for a couple of nights at home. However, as soon as he stepped off the boat, we recognised him and ran to meet him.

We chattered excitedly on the way back to Granda's.

"I'm going to the pictures," I said.

"Oh," said Dad, "what's on?"

"A western," I replied. "I don't know if Auntie Etta is going." She often went, and sometimes I came to Burra on my own for a weekend so I could go too.

"What about tomorrow?" Dad asked. "Do you know your words?"

"Mam brought them with her," I said.

After teatime, I got ready to go to the pictures. Auntie Etta decided she wouldn't come this time, but I didn't mind going on my own. Dad gave me the money and I set off.

There was already a good crowd in, when I got to the hall, but I went right to the front and found a seat with Marjory and Ann and lots of other girls.

I looked round in my seat. Unlike what happened in Scalloway, there was no projector standing in the aisle. Instead, there was a special projection box high up in the ceiling and, when I looked up, I could see Walter Leask from the Point moving about in there. He even showed the films when it was the Highlands and Islands' turn, so Geordie Horne never came to Burra.

Soon the lights dimmed, the audience fell silent and the screen lit up. The pictures were good. Just as in Scalloway, there was a whole programme of films before the main one which was quite loud in parts with lots of shooting and horses galloping, but it all worked out in the end and I hurried home. Mam had told me to come straight back as I'd need my sleep before tomorrow.

The next afternoon, faces newly washed, we set off to catch Lowrie's bus. We needed to go by bus because the chapel wasn't in Hamnavoe; it was at the Toogs, which was a long way to walk, especially with a suitcase.

Auntie Janie and Auntie Jessie were already on the bus, and Annie, Auntie Mimie's mother, along with some other people. There was room for us, but it wasn't a big bus and Lowrie said he'd have to do a second run. He didn't have a timetable like the Scalloway buses to Lerwick, but then he wasn't a full-time bus driver either. Usually when we saw Lowrie, he was working in his family's shop along with his brother and sister, Robbie and Teenie.

When we got to the chapel and everyone clambered out, most passengers went straight into the church by the front porch, but not us.

"We have to meet the others in the vestry," I said.

"That's right," said Mam, "I'm coming with you."

The vestry was open, but there was no-one else there yet. Mam got out her comb, tidied our hair and we sat down. We hadn't waited long when we heard running feet and the door burst open. Excited children poured in along with our teachers and some helpers.

Amid the commotion, places were found for coats, combs were wet to slick back hair, socks were pulled up evenly and collars straightened. Meanwhile, two men came in, carrying between them the large model of a fishing boat that

Scalloway Sunday school anniversary

A seven-foot model of a seine net fishing boat against a deep blue backcloth emblazoned with a red cross and the words "Fishers of Men" was the striking centre-piece on the platform of the Scalloway Methodist Church at the annual Sunday School anniversary on Sunday evening.

The boat, one-tenth scale of a 70 foot seine netter, was built by the senior boys' bible class. At the beginning of the service only the hull of the boat was on the platform but as the children sang and spoke of the equipment needed for the voyage of life, so the appropriate piece of gear was added to the construction of the vessel.

The church was packed when Rev H. R. Bowes introduced the service and led opening devotions. The boat and her crew were described in a scripture reading of Jesus gathering His crew read by Tommy Watt, chorus by the children, "I will make you fishers of men," and a recitation "Fishermen of Galilee" by Robt. Stewart. Nets were piled on the deck of the boat after Margaret Watt had read the scripture lesson telling how the nets were filled, and the congregation joined in the singing of "Hear us, O Lord, from heaven, Thy dwelling place."

Before the wheel and wheelhouse was constructed Arnold Duncan read the Pilot Psalm by Capt. J. H. Roberts, and the children's choir sang "Stay I rise, may I rise, at the break of the day." The necessity of a compass and direction finder was revealed in two narratives by Jimmy Watt and Mary Thomson. Up went her masts and derricks next and Jim Stewart read a narration on "The masts." Louise Gray on "The mizzen sail" and a scripture reading by Robert Smith "Landing the catch."

Lifesaving gear was needed for a safe voyage and after Tommy Georgeson had read a narrative on that theme and a scripture reading about the storm on Galilee a lifebelt was placed on the side of the wheelhouse. Beginners and primary pupils sang "Peter's little brown boat." Continuing on this theme a sextet sang "Fierce raged the tempest"—Rena Fraser, Marie Georgeson, Iris Morrison, Mary Thomson, Cathie Watt and Margaret Watt; the scripture reading describing the storm in the Mediterranean was read by Cathie Watt; and Rena Fraser and Marie Georgeson recited "Lord in the hollow of Thy hand."

Church lights were dimmed as the children sang "When darkness creeps over the sea" and after John Moore read a narrative "The ship's lights" the navigation lights winked on and the choir recited "The Lord is my light and my salvation." Scripture sentences on this theme were read by two Sunday School teachers, the congregation joined in the singing of "O Jesus, King most wonderful."

Aerials were strung from mast to mast to wheelhouse after Jim Stewart had emphasised the need for communication with the shore and the fleet; the scripture reading, O that men would praise the Lord, was read by Valerie Slater, and the choir sang "Far round the world Thy children sing their song." Her name, port of origin, and registration were revealed in a narrative by Phyllis Gray, Billy Watt, Donnie Nicolson, and Katherine Goodlad. When they had done this they revealed the name "Scalloway" on the stern, "Christian" on the wheelhouse and lifebelt, and "NJ 153 Christian" on the bow. NJ represented New Jerusalem the port of destination, and 153 was the number of fish caught by the Galilean fishermen, this article to be added to the

boats gear was the anchor. Its importance was shown by a narration by Thelma Ridland followed by the congregational hymn "Will your anchor hold in the storms of life."

After the collection had been taken up by four scholars, certificates were presented to teachers and pupils who were successful in a recent Old Testament examination. Before pronouncing the benediction Mr Bowes expressed the hope that everyone had received a message and a blessing from the service.

Organist throughout the service was Miss Eileen Moore. The children will travel to the Burra Isle Methodist Chapel next Sunday to give the same demonstration service there.

Report from *The Shetland Times* of 6th June, 1958.

was the centrepiece of this year's service. John Macdonald called for quiet and asked us not to make a sound while the door to the church was opened so the boat could be taken through. When that was done, he lined us up in the order we would be sitting and we went through to take our places.

Robina and I sat together at the end of a row, near to the vestry door. The church was packed and, from where we sat, we could see everyone in the congregation. I knew lots of people, and recognised others I'd seen there before, but whose names I didn't know.

The boat was over to our left, high up in the pulpit where it could be seen from the pews, exactly as it had been in Scalloway. At this stage, it was no more than an anonymous brown hull, but as the service went on, various Sunday School pupils, helped by members of the Bible Class, added the wheelhouse, masts and nets, and all the other things fishermen required to do their job properly.

When it was time to reveal the name and number, I had to ask Mr Bowes, the minister, what the number was. He then told the congregation it was one-five-three which was the number of fish the disciples caught in the Sea of Galilee. After that, I had to unveil the name of the boat and that meant going up into the pulpit. There wasn't much room getting past everyone, but, once there, the piece of brown-painted card covering the name on the front of the wheelhouse came away easily in my hand to reveal the name, *Christian*. The last bit of equipment to be added was the anchor when everyone sang 'Will Your Anchor Hold'. After that, we had 'Eternal Father' and then the benediction.

Right after the service, we filed back into the vestry where our teachers helped us find our coats. Mam turned up to help us before we made our way round to where Dad was speaking to someone at the chapel door. There was no sign of our aunts; they must have already left for Hamnavoe. Dad had charge of the suitcase as we went with the rest of the Sunday School party down the brae away from the church.

Soon, we came to the house where Nurse Pratt lived. A big cheery woman, she was the district nurse and Mam said she'd brought me into the world. The pier down below her house was known as the nurse's pier and that's where the *Tirrick* would be waiting for us. The *Tirrick* didn't usually come to the Toogs, but the Sunday School always hired her specially for the occasion.

It had been a short visit to Burra this time, but in another few weeks, the school would close for the summer and we'd be back.

CHAPTER TWENTY-TWO

Treasure Hunt

Swimsuits, bathing hats and towels lay on the kitchen table.
"Go and get your buckets and spades," Mam said, holding out
the key to the shed. We didn't linger; this was the day of the Sunday
School picnic.

"I'm pleased it's St Ninian's Isle," I said to Mam as I returned the key.
It was already my favourite place for this particular outing, but I was
especially pleased to be going there again this year. We'd heard about an
excavation by students and the discovery, by a Lerwick boy, of treasure in
the ruins of the old kirk on the island.

"Some don't like it," Mam said, breaking into my thoughts, "they
think it's too far."

I knew what she was getting at: the long drive meant there was
more chance of children being sick on the bus, but I had other
preoccupations.

"Will we see the treasure?" I asked.

"They'll have taken it away," Mam replied.

"But there might be more," I said, "maybe we'll find some if we look."

"Maybe," said Mam, in the way of adults expressing doubt.

While we'd been speaking, she'd packed our swimming things
along with her makkin into a bag and was ready to leave. On the
way out, Robina and I retrieved our buckets and spades from where
we'd left them beside the back steps and waited while Mam locked
the door and placed the key under the stone on top of the coal box
behind the house.

From St Ninian's Isle.

At the chapel, Georgeson and Moore's bus was drawing up outside, the driver careful to avoid the crowd of youngsters spilling off the narrow pavements. Once he'd brought the bus to a halt, the driver got out and closed the door behind him; no-one was allowed on board yet.

From the open vestry door, a stream of Sunday School teachers and helpers had emerged, carrying food and the other paraphernalia necessary for the success of the day, all of which the driver then helped them stow in the lockers underneath the bus.

In the meantime, Mam directed us to where a group of youngsters and their mothers waited by the church porch. Conversation was exchanged regarding the weather and the trip ahead until finally the bus door opened and we joined the throng of youngsters, each of us intent on securing the best seat.

Robina and I managed to get a seat halfway along the bus while various adults helped stow our belongings in the overhead shelf. The grown-ups sat nearer the front, though I did notice they left the very front seat, beside the door, empty. On the long drive, there was only one stop and a single white-faced picnicker to claim that front seat before the bus eventually came to a halt in Bigton.

In an aisle crowded with excitement and anticipation, Robina and I were reunited with our bits and pieces before leaving the bus to join our mother on the path to the sands. For me, the appeal of St Ninian's Isle had always been great. First, there was the novelty of being able to reach an island on foot – St Ninian's Isle was connected to the mainland by a wide stretch of sand – then there was the sea which lapped along the two long sides of the ayre, creating the illusion of two beaches in one. But this year, it seemed to me, all that was surpassed by news of treasure and the possibilities that now arose. Was there more to be found?

I could wait no longer and ran on ahead. I wasn't alone; at the foot of the path a group of children was gathering, a sign that the usual sprint across the sands was imminent. This was not a race; it was a ritual – races would come later. We'd reached the sands, now it was time to claim the isle. Abandoning my bucket and spade, I joined the group.

There was no signal and no need for one; as the last stragglers reached us we moved forward. At first, my feet slipped and slid uncomfortably in the dry sand, but those of us who'd done this before understood the choice we faced and, in the company of several others, I soon veered off towards the water. I knew this diversion would add to the distance we must cover, but I quickly became aware of the benefit underfoot as my feet made contact with the firmer sand closer to the sea edge.

Confident now that I could move more easily, I allowed myself to take in more of the scene. Over to my left, those who'd chosen to make straight across the middle of the sands stumbled on, still slightly in front of us. Ahead, the sea edge curved inwards, narrowing the ayre for part of its length before sweeping outwards again to where the sand spread itself along the shore of the flat, green island beyond.

It was tempting to stay close to the water, but as soon as the shoreline began arching away from us, I knew it was time to change direction. St Ninian's Isle was fringed with low cliffs of dark rock apart from one area, roughly midway along the far end of the sands, where the island's hard edge softened to allow a way up to the grassy top. Turning away from the sea, my running companions and I now headed towards the start of this path.

As the smooth sand gave way to a dry unevenness, our feet once again struggled on the shifting surface, but with the end in sight, that no longer mattered quite as much. Reunited with those who'd taken the shorter route, we paused at the foot of the steep path to get our breath back. From that position, it was hard to see what was going on at the other side of the sands, but I did glance over to try and work out where Mam had gone. She'd have found a sheltered spot by now and was probably already engaged in her knitting. I'd see better from the isle.

After the long run, it was hard-going up the sandy path, but there was no giving up now. At the top, solid ground awaited and I stepped with some relief onto the familiar short grass with its smattering of wild flowers. Now I could think more seriously about the ruined kirk and its treasure, our intended destination ever since we'd begun gathering for our run across the sands.

No trip to St Ninian's Isle was complete without an opportunity to visit these ruins, not that there was much left of the old church, just an open doorway through which we could step onto a grassy floor bounded by thick stone walls that weren't high enough to contain windows or support a roof. However, the site did hold a fascination for me that neither Scalloway Castle nor Jarlshof allowed: here we had the freedom to explore unsupervised, to rebuild the kirk in our minds, to position pews and pulpit, to wonder once more who'd traipse across the sands to services. Had they had a Sunday School? Mam would've had something to say if we'd had to cross these sands in our best shoes. And this year there was the added wonder created by having played there while there was treasure under our feet; it was just like a storybook – and I couldn't persuade myself there was no more treasure to be found.

From the top of the path, it wasn't far to the ruins so I heard immediately the cries of dismay from the first youngsters to reach the site. Our way into the old kirk was blocked. A fence had been erected with a gate that was firmly locked. How dare they? Today, the island was ours. The ruins too.

I went right up to the fence and looked in, but it was hard to recognise the place. I could make out the roughly rectangular shape formed by the walls, but the ground was scattered with digging equipment and wooden boards which presumably covered the spots where the ground had been dug up. So much for looking for more treasure.

After initial expressions of disappointment and not a little anger, our gang fell silent, with some picnickers beginning to head back to the sands. Casting my eye over the ground just in case there would be signs of treasures untold, I moved away from the offending fence to a spot where I had a good view back the way we'd come.

By now, Mam would be looking out for signs of life at the old kirk. The walls, moss-covered and with grass growing out the top, were low enough

Mam, Sunday School Superintendent John Macdonald, and Georgie Duthie. In the background to the right are Robina (in dark shorts) and myself (with arm raised).

Photo courtesy of Elizabeth Marshall

for us to scramble onto and be seen by parents and teachers. Mam would be expecting the customary enthusiastic wave from that position; would she notice a half-hearted effort from my new vantage point?

Below me, the sea sparkled in the sun, the wet sand close to the sea edge shone like a mirror and I could make out movement at the other side of the sands. The first children to leave the isle now appeared below me, no longer running, but walking in small groups till, occasionally, one or two would break away and head for the sea, removing socks and shoes as they went. The delighted screams as their toes encountered the water reached me, but I couldn't share their joy.

This was most likely my last Sunday School picnic at St Ninian's Isle. Next year would be my very last one before I moved up to the Bible Class, but we'd not come here on two consecutive trips; it would be either the Meal Saands or Gulberwick. Meal was somewhere I went each summer during family visits to Burra and, though there was the prospect of building a dam across the burn at Gulberwick, it couldn't hold the same appeal for me as St Ninian's Isle did.

There was nothing for it; I turned to follow the last of our party now making their way back. At the foot of the path, I stopped to remove my sandals and ankle socks. I'd be heading across the middle of the sands and that was easier with bare feet.

CHAPTER TWENTY-THREE

Summer's End

K ulla, kulla, kulla, kulla ...
I looked up from my book. On the roof of the house, a line of maas was making its presence felt, each bird apparently intent on outdoing the others in the stridency of its tone and the exuberance of its movement. I wondered yet again how they kept their feet as, heads thrown back and noisy beaks projected skyward, they repeatedly dipped down to a nodding stop then arched up again to rejoin the raucous choir.

"Greetin' for rain," Mam would say about this behaviour. I shivered, but not entirely due to the thought of rain; the sun had been off the back green for some time and I knew it would soon be disappearing altogether behind the wast hill. I closed my book, laid it to the side, picked up the stool I'd been sitting on and was about to replace it in the shed when I heard the click of the front gate and footsteps on the path.

I turned. It was Dad, back from the pier, his presence marking more than an impending teatime; it was a sure sign of a change of season. The herring fishing was over and, one by one, the boats were returning from the east side. As the herring began their move south to warmer waters, the men came ashore for a couple of weeks to settle their accounts and begin plans for the winter fishing. I put the stool into the shed, closed the door and followed Dad into the house.

At teatime, Mam told us she would be taking Robina and me to the Lerwick shops tomorrow. "There are things to get before you can go back to school," she said.

Dad's news was that he'd arranged to spread the herring nets on

Da Cupps, an area of grass not far from the pier. Now, this promised to be more interesting than a shopping trip – including the chance of a run home on the back of a lorry.

For the herring fishing, individual members of the crew provided a number of nets each. Those were made of cotton and rigged so they'd hang vertically in the sea to form a curtain through which the smaller fish could pass, but not the bigger ones. On occasion, Dad told us, small sharks – hoes he called them – got trapped in the nets, causing a lot of damage in their struggle to free themselves. That, and other wear and tear had to be repaired, a job that mostly fell to the womenfolk. However, before they could make a start, the nets had to have the salt removed from them by being spread out flat in a field in the hope that enough rain would fall and wash them clean.

"From the carry-on of the maas on the roof this afternoon," Mam said, "you might not have long to wait for a downpour."

Dad agreed, then added, "There are no sheep on Da Cupps just now; we'll get the nets spread tomorrow."

"Can we help?" I wondered.

"I thought Mam said you were going to Lerwick," was Dad's reply.

"That's right;" Mam added, "the holidays will soon be over."

After tea, instead of letting us out to play, Mam had us trying on school clothes to see what still fitted, what we'd outgrown, which items of mine Robina should now wear, and what had to be replaced.

The next morning was dull and overcast as the three of us boarded the ten o'clock bus to Lerwick. As the bus toiled up the Scord, I looked over to the pier where one of Johnson's brown lorries was parked close to where some fishing boats were tied up. I couldn't see clearly what was going on, but men did seem to be busy round the lorry – loading nets perhaps. From the appearance of the sky, it wouldn't be too long before any nets that were spread would be thoroughly clean.

It was already raining when we got to Lerwick so I followed closely as Mam took a firm hold of Robina's hand and hurried us along Commercial Street to the shelter of D & G Kay's draper's shop. Despite the weather, there were already several customers inside, waiting at one or other of two long counters that ran the full length of the shop floor, from front to back. In behind the counters were polished wooden shelves and drawers from which we watched assistants expertly select various items of clothing calculated to meet with their customers' approval.

When it was our turn, Mam asked about a skirt for me, so we were shown through to the changing room in the back shop. Next on Mam's list was a blouse for each of us, then it was back to the counter where our assistant brought us warm vests, navy knickers, knee socks and those horrible long brown stockings that Mam insisted we wear in the winter. But worst of all, to hold them up, we also had to buy warm-lined liberty bodices to which we'd later attach clumsy button-on suspenders.

Once we'd got everything, the assistant went over to the large roll of brown wrapping paper that was fixed on to the end of the counter and unrolled what she judged would be enough to contain our purchases. Next, she reached for a spool of flat, papery string on which was printed the name of the shop. Once the parcel was tied up, she carefully labelled it and put it aside for us to collect later.

Our next visit was to lower Goodlad's shoe shop. Even blindfolded, we'd have known which shop we were in, so overwhelming was the smell of leather. As usual, we were shown through to the room on the left where there were wooden chairs, a footstool to assist in the trying on of shoes and a square of carpet in the middle of the stone floor. We were surrounded by boxes and boxes of shoes, but I knew we'd get little chance to see inside them; we were there for brown lacing Clark's shoes that would soon take the place of the Clark's sandals we'd worn all summer. That left time for a cup of tea and a chocolate biscuit before picking up our parcels in time to catch the one o'clock bus home.

The bus was busy with several families on the same expedition and it smelled of damp clothes and damp paper from the many parcels in the overhead shelf or heaped up on the two front seats. While the adults on board involved themselves in the usual conversation about how quickly holidays go, how the nights were already drawing in and how well, or otherwise, the herring fishing had gone, my thoughts returned to the business of the nets.

They'd be spread by now, but that wasn't the end of the story. In recent summers, we'd been around to watch the lifting of the nets – and enjoy being taken home on the back of a lorry loaded with nets – but apart from that, I was now wondering if Dad would let me help. Surely I was old enough. Individually, the nets weren't that heavy; I'd seen how easily the men handled them.

I was glad Dad hadn't had to wait long for the necessary rain, though it was a nuisance as far as our usual activities were concerned.

As if reading my mind, Robina said, "I'd wanted to go swimming this afternoon."

"Don't think we'd be allowed;" I replied, "it's too wet." We giggled at that idea.

"Shame," Robina said, "there won't be many more chances."

It was raining heavily in Scalloway as we got off the bus and hurried into the house. We removed our coats, but, before hanging them up, took them to the back door where Mam gave them a good shake in the hope of removing some of the wet,

"At least your father'll be pleased," she said, as we placed the sodden coats on hangers.

"He'll soon be looking for better weather, though," I replied, "so the nets can dry again. When do you think they'll be ready for lifting?"

Whether or not Mam realised I was hoping to help out, I couldn't tell. "We'll have to listen to the forecast," was all she would say.

Next morning, when I looked out from the bedroom window, roofs were darker, grass and shrubs brighter and, along the underside of the clothes line, a necklace of raindrops glistened in a watery sun, but at least the rain had stopped falling.

Over on Da Cupps I could make out rectangular patches of brown netting, made visible because there were too many nets to be spread out singly so several had been laid one on top of another. This arrangement clearly required the arrival of a stronger sun to effect the drying.

Over the next few days, the weather did steadily improve till the skies cleared, patches of damp disappeared from the roads, the pavements dried up and the grass invited us to take a seat in the sunshine, but more importantly, the nets were declared dry.

"Can I help with the lifting?" I asked Dad.

"And me?" Robina wasn't going to be left out.

"You're too peerie," Dad said.

"What about me?" I asked again.

"We'll have to see when we get there."

That was good enough for me and I went looking for Mam to find out which old clothes I should wear.

"Watch where you're putting your feet," Dad said, as I took my place in a line of helpers spread out alongside one batch of nets. Working together, we picked up the edge of the top net and walked forward while gathering

A piece of herring net, corks and needle.

the rest of it into our outstretched arms. We moved carefully, to avoid disturbing or tripping over, the remaining nets underfoot. Once we were safely across, one of the men took charge of the long loose roll of netting, ossils, rope and corks that was the result of our labours, folded it up and tied it into a tight bundle, while the rest of us got ready to tackle the next one. I felt so proud.

When all the nets had been piled onto the back of a lorry, Robina and I were helped on board and allowed to snuggle down among them, for the run home. Once the lorry was parked at our gate and everyone had dismounted safely, the men began carrying the nets, one at a time, on their backs, along the path to the shed where Mam and Auntie Jessie would carry out the mending.

We kept out of the way till the lorry had gone when Robina and I had a look in the shed. After they'd been mended, the herring nets would be stored in the loft of the shed, but for now Dad was ensuring they were secure where they'd been piled up against the wooden partition that divided the downstairs part into two.

"Have you put any through to the other room?" I asked.

"One or two," Dad said.

Curiosity not quite satisfied, I moved over to where he was working and clicked open the door to the inner room. Robina followed me. In

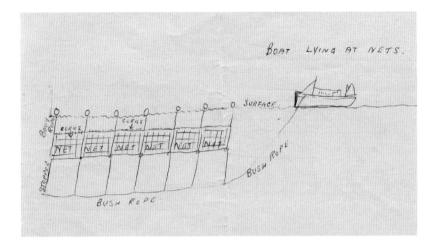

To start with, a herring net is 55 yards long by 17 yards deep, with corks on the upper rope.

A fleet of nets are from 70 to 100 nets, and they are all tied together in a length, they reach from a mile to a mile and a half.

There is a bowy on each net with a rope about 3 fathoms long and a stopper on the lower leg and that is tied to a heavy rope while the nets are being shot. They are all shot by hand by two men standing close together and hanking them over the side of the boat while the boat is going slow before the wind.

The boat is then turned head to wind and when it is time to haul again the heavy rope (you have heard about a bush rope) is laid on the

winch and the boat is heaved up along the nets and they are pulled in by hand and the herrings shaken out on to the deck, they then go down hatches on the deck into the hold.

When they are all hauled then the boat goes full speed for the port to get them sold. Sometimes the nets have to be hauled on to the deck to clean out any that might still be sticking in the net. That is done on the way ashore.

The modern way of fishing is with the purse-net, it is shot around the shoal and then drawn together to form a purse with the herrings all swimming inside it, the meshes are too small for the fish to mesh, then they are pumped onboard.

Drift netting for herring. Diagram and descriptions by my father, Willie Goodlad.

here, the outside walls were lined with wood, and a paraffin heater stood close to the partition. Under the window, the sturdy wooden chairs where Mam and Auntie Jessie would sit were already in place. There was also a clean wooden fish box lying on its side where it too could be used as a seat. Fastened to the wall opposite the chairs was the pulley used by the women to hoist the nets upwards as they worked. The nets Dad had mentioned lay on the floor, below where the pulley hung.

From this side, the wooden framework of the partition was visible, part of it forming a handy shelf on which lay the net mending needles. I picked one of those up and turned it over in my hand. It wasn't like an ordinary needle; it was much bigger, and flat, and not made from metal. At one end it tapered to a point, and at the other end, it curved inwards. It didn't have the sort of eye you'd see in a conventional needle, instead it was largely open towards the pointed end and within this outsize eye was a thin spike.

Two balls of twine and some scissors lay beside the needles. Robina had picked up a needle as well and we both knew what to do. Later, we'd earn extra pocket money by filling the needles, but for now it was more of a game, a novelty. I began as usual by wrapping the end of the twine round the spike a few times till I felt it would hold, then I drew it along one of the flat sides with the intention of flipping the needle as I passed the twine round its concave end.

Instead of turning cleanly, the needle slipped from my hand and ended up on the floor, the twine unravelling as it fell. I picked it up, tidied up the ball of twine and began again, this time successfully turning the needle while persuading the reluctant twine round its curved end and along the flat side that was now uppermost. Keeping the twine taut, I then wrapped it, just once this time, round the spike. I breathed more easily, but there was still a long way to go. It was a matter of once more flipping the needle while passing the thread round the curved end and back to the spike.

The idea was to repeat these movements till the spike was almost covered in twine when the needle could be declared full. By the time I'd finished, my fingers were quite cramped – and Robina had disappeared. I used the scissors to cut the twine and placed the filled needle alongside the scissors and the now depleted ball on the narrow shelf where I'd found them.

The next day, Mam was busy in the spare bedroom. I went up to see what she was doing.

"Auntie Jessie'll be here soon," she said.

"When?" I asked.

"Just as soon as you go back to school."

After school, the first day back, I came home to a locked door. There was no sign of Robina, but I let myself in using the key from under the large stone on top of the coal box. Robina's schoolbag was in the living room and I put mine down beside it. I might not know where my sister was, but I knew where to find Mam and went out to the shed.

"Where's Robina?" I asked, as I opened the door to the inner room,

"With Hazel," Mam said, "now go and get changed. You can't come in here in your school clothes."

Hazel was in Robina's class at school and lived further up the road. I did as I was told, and got back as quickly as I could. Mam and Auntie Jessie were busy working on a net. On the narrow shelf beside them were balls of twine and needles: some full, some empty. Beside the women was a tally of the number of lengths they'd worked. I watched for a bit as they wove the needles in and out, stopping every so often to snip the twine with the small scissors they managed to keep hold of throughout.

I picked up an empty needle and flipped it round in my hand; it didn't fall to the floor. The paraffin heater was lit and the room was warm. I sat down on the fish box, reached for a ball of twine and began to fill the needle.

No doubt now. It was summer's end.

Postscript

From the time I left school in the mid-1960s until 2004, most of my life was spent outwith the islands, but wherever I lived, Shetland was always hame. Having had a lifelong interest in writing, I made several attempts at creating something based on my life in Shetland, but it was only with the birth of my nieces in the 1980s that I began to concentrate on writing about the childhood their mother, Robina, and I had experienced in Shetland.

The girls were born three years apart, the same age difference as that between Robina and me, but rather than dwell on such similarities, I was immediately struck by the contrast in circumstances. Whereas I had been born on an island with neither running water nor electricity, my newborn nieces could look forward to a childhood in the affluent middle-class west end of Glasgow.

Many children who have a parent from Shetland will experience regular family holidays in the islands, where they get to know not only something of the way of life, but also the people to whom they are connected. As it turns out, this represents another contrast in the lives of my sister and her children when considered alongside those of other family members who lived sooth: various cousins whose children spent time each year with Shetland grandparents. Sadly for my nieces, there were to be reduced opportunities for getting to know the extended family, for getting a feel for island life: my father passed away before the girls were born and my mother died not long before my younger niece's first birthday.

By the 1980s, the way of life Robina and I had experienced had disappeared, but even without the catalyst of having nieces born and brought up in the circumstances I've described, I felt that the memory of a long gone lifestyle was intrinsically worth preserving. My contribution therefore was to write little stories for the girls that illustrated just how different life had been for their mother and me.

But how to tackle it. For the girls, I invented a character named Janet who had a younger sister and wrote about them both, but in the third person. My nieces enjoyed those fictionalised accounts which I continued to produce for a number of years. This gave me the idea to expand the work into something with a wider appeal and, for a time, I continued with the made-up family, even inventing an island group for their home.

Then in the early 1990s, I read a newspaper article about The Arvon Foundation, an organisation that offers "people time and space to write, with an annual programme of residential courses and retreats". I applied soon afterwards and, over the years, attended several courses, learning from the wit, wisdom and experience of professional writers.

After that, it was up to me.

The result is not autobiography; though I feature throughout, it isn't even about me. It's more a glimpse into the past where I set out to describe events through the eyes of the child that I believe I might have been, as they happened and without resorting to hindsight.

Though eschewing autobiography, I aimed for a more or less chronological approach, with flashbacks when mentioning anything that had affected the family, either before I was born or when I was too young to remember. But having a plan, still left me with lots of decisions to make, many of them relating to how I should work real people into the writing.

How fair, for instance, would it be to name people? On the other hand, could I realistically describe an event or occasion without mentioning names? How much should I say about those whose names I felt had to be included? Which words, if any, should I put in their mouths? Because of the difficulties of putting words into the mouths of others, how much could I get off with if I avoided direct speech?

And the biggest questions of all: how would anyone feel about being mentioned – and how might they feel about not being mentioned?

I had no compunction about naming certain relatives: my immediate family, my grandfather, aunts, uncles and various cousins, but in order to recreate a way of life, I had to go beyond the family. My good friend Vivian gave me her blessing to include her by name. Also named are a neighbour, the butcher, shop assistants, our Sunday School superintendent, the *Tirrick*'s boatman, stars of variety concerts, various teachers and people too close to the story being told to be left out, for example the minister ('A Short Visit') and the skipper of the *Jessie Sinclair* ('Winning Ways').

Perhaps the most basic question I had to address was the one concerning exactly which aspects of 1950s' life to include. But even when I had decided on a topic, there were other questions to face, the most pressing of which related to people. Where the subject was a family matter, I found it straightforward enough, but writing about community events was trickier. For one thing, I couldn't always be sure exactly who was involved on particular occasions. Rather than make such things up, I therefore had to find ways of writing round gaps in my memory.

Questions of who and what weren't the only ones requiring resolution, I also had to consider how. There's many a truth revealed in fiction and I'd certainly been persuaded to adopt a creative framework, while sticking as closely as possible to verifiable fact. The answer to this conundrum had to be creative non-fiction.

That decision came easily enough, its execution anything but, as I entered the war between content and style, truth and fact. How to resolve it?

My solution was to incorporate more than one memory into a single piece of writing. 'Special Delivery' is a good example. The chapter describes the day my father took me to Lerwick to pick up my mother and my new baby sister. I was only three years old and yet have a very clear memory of seeing my mother emerge from the 'Annexe' with a nurse who was holding the baby. I also remember details of a conversation in the car about names – in fact, I remember more of what was said than I have included. After discussing the baby's and my mother's names, my father told me that his name, Willie, was the same as one of my names, Williamina, but I left that out as 'Special Delivery' was intended as a celebration of my peerie sister.

So far, so non-fiction. Where the creativity comes in is in the rest of that chapter, especially the description of a drive to Lerwick and the conversation with Hindie Johnson, neither of which I remember from that particular day. I'm not even sure who the driver was on that occasion.

So why did I feel able to include those things? The answer is simply that the journey between Scalloway and Lerwick, more usually by bus, was to become a very familiar one to me, and being teased by Hindie about exchanging my sister for a car, was a regular occurrence in the years to come.

I've been asked to give more explanation as to who some of the characters, such as Hindie, were. Hindie was one of three brothers who ran J. Johnson & Sons in Scalloway. They ran buses between Scalloway and Lerwick and had a fleet of lorries; and cars that could be hired, with a driver, for special occasions.

Uncle Hancie was Hancie Smith, who ran a ferry service between Scalloway and Hamnavoe from 28th July, 1947 until October 1971 when the bridges to Trondra and Burra were opened. He was my mother's elder brother. Andrew who worked for him was Andrew Henry, a Foula man who lived in Scalloway.

I feel that anyone else mentioned, whether Dr Durham or Teenie working in Christie's shop in Hamnavoe, are sufficiently defined by their appearance in the book as that was how I saw them as a child and did not know them at any other level.

I make one exception: my peerie sister. Robina did well for herself in the world of academia, being granted a personal chair at Glasgow University as Professor of Housing and Urban Studies. Sadly, in 2005, she became terminally ill and passed away in June of that year leaving behind a husband and two daughters, and many other grieving relatives. Before she died, she requested that something I had written be read out at her funeral. I chose 'Special Delivery' and read it myself to a crowded Glasgow University Chapel.

That last sad reflection apart, I trust that the result of my deliberations in the preparation of this book is that I have managed to convey something of the character of the way of life I knew as a child. There are many more stories that could be told of the post-war era in Shetland and I hope those can yet be articulated, if not by me, then by some of you...

Glossary of Terms

ayre	*isthmus*
but	*living room*
cloo	*ball of wool*
closs	(noun) *close, a passage between buildings*
denner	*main meal of the day, traditionally eaten at 1pm*
geo	*small, steep inlet*
gruel	*porridge*
hame	*home*
hoe	*dogfish*
LHD	*fishing boat agents (Lowestoft Herring Drifters)*
loop	*stitch in knitting*
maa	*adult seagull*
makk	*knit; I use both these words interchangeably*
makkin	*knitting; I use both these words interchangeably*
ossils	*thin pieces of rope that form part of the border of a herring net*
peerie	*an indispensable Shetland dialect word meaning small, little or young*
pirm	*reel, as of thread*
planticrub	*small, circular dry stone enclosure for seedlings*
redd	(verb) *tidy*
rig	*plot of land for cultivation*
sassermaet	*a type of sausagemeat, produced by Shetland butchers*
sooth	*south, but also used as a noun to refer to the UK mainland*
spent	(noun) *a fish that has spawned*
spoot	*razor clam*
the Street	*Main Street, Scalloway*
swinkle	(verb) *used of water and the sound it makes when moving inside a container*
tatties	*potatoes*
tyals	*a fastening, such as on a bonnet with strips of material for tying*
wast	*west*
wire	*knitting needle*
yoag	*horse mussel*

A Shetland Childhood

Biography

Catherine was born in Burra, brought up in Scalloway and attended secondary school in Lerwick before heading south. After graduating with an MA from Aberdeen University and gaining a post-graduate teaching certificate at Aberdeen College of Education, she taught for almost thirty years in schools large and small, in primary and in secondary education, in state and in private schools, in mainstream, learning support and in special needs. That was mainly in Scotland, but included a year in Australia under the exchange programme for Commonwealth teachers.

In her own time, she obtained from the Open University, degree-level qualifications in computing that allowed her to train staff in educational software as well as to teach pupils. Aged 50, she sought other employment that could make use of those skills, working in business and in finance for Thomas Rogerson & Sons and The National Trust for Scotland.

Throughout her life, she has maintained an interest in writing and, on returning to Shetland, wrote a weekly column for *The Shetland Times*, giving that up after two years, to concentrate on the contents of this book.

She has had several pieces of writing published in *The New Shetlander* magazine.